THE LIFE AND TIMES OF TAKABUTI
IN ANCIENT EGYPT

THE LIFE AND TIMES OF TAKABUTI IN ANCIENT EGYPT

INVESTIGATING THE BELFAST MUMMY

EDITED BY

ROSALIE DAVID AND EILEEN MURPHY

LIVERPOOL UNIVERSITY PRESS

RD – To Mrs Kay Bellinger and Mr J. H. Davidson in gratitude for many years of support for research endeavours in the KNH Centre for Biomedical Egyptology, University of Manchester and to Mr J. Yendle for his much valued technological advice.

EM – To all those who have been fascinated by Takabuti since her arrival in Belfast in 1834.

First published 2021 by
Liverpool University Press
4 Cambridge Street
Liverpool
L69 7ZU

British Library Cataloguing-in-Publication data
A British Library CIP record is available

ISBN 978-1-80034-858-5

Typeset by Carnegie Book Production, Lancaster
Printed in the Czech Republic via Akcent Media Limited

Cover image: The line of hieroglyphs shown on the cover is from a painted horizontal band of inscription on Takabuti's wooden coffin. Read from left to right, they spell out her name. According to ancient Egyptian belief, inclusion of a name identified ownership of the coffin, and helped to ensure that the deceased person attained eternal life. The cover, designed by Libby Mulqueeny, Queen's University Belfast, shows the head of Takabuti's coffin (Dynasty 25), National Museum NI, Collection Ulster Museum. It also features the latest facial reconstruction of Takabuti created by Caroline Wilkinson and Sarah Shrimpton, Liverpool John Moores University.

Contents

Contributors

The late Judith Adams was Professor of Diagnostic Radiology, Clinical Radiology, Imaging Science and Biomedical Engineering in the Faculty of Medicine at the University of Manchester. She led the programme of radiological studies undertaken by the Manchester Mummy Research Project after joining the team in 1998, and published work in this field.

Davide Chiasserini is Assistant Professor of Biochemistry at the University of Perugia, Italy. He holds an MSc in Biological Sciences and a PhD in Neuroscience. He has extensive experience in proteome analytical techniques, including high-resolution mass spectrometry, chromatography and multiplex immunoassays, acquired in several laboratories across Europe, mainly in Italy, the Netherlands, Sweden and the UK. He has a keen interest in the global analysis of protein expression in biological samples and biofluids, especially in neurodegenerative disorders and cancer. The main lines of investigation in which he engages are quantitative mass spectrometry applied to the field of biomarkers research, validation of analytical methods for protein biomarkers in biological fluids, and studies of protein aggregation properties in biological samples.

Rosalie David is Professor Emerita of Egyptology and co-director of the KNH Centre for Biomedical Egyptology at the University of Manchester. She has been the director of the Manchester Mummy Project since its inception in 1973, and has established biomedical Egyptology as a new university specialisation, to provide a different approach to understanding ancient Egyptian civilisation. She has lectured around the world, is the author/editor of over 30 books and many papers in academic journals, and has been consultant/contributor for television documentaries. In

2003 she was awarded an OBE for services to Egyptology, and has received Fellowships of the Royal Society of Arts and the Royal Society of Medicine.

Konstantina Drosou is a lecturer at the KNH Centre for Biomedical Egyptology at the University of Manchester. She studied archaeology in Greece, and went on to do an MSc in Archaeological Sciences at the University of Bradford, and a PhD in Evolutionary Biology at the University of Manchester. After completing a two-year postdoctoral position, she was awarded the position of lecturer in Biomedical Egyptology. She has worked as a field osteoarchaeologist in Greece, Spain and Romania, and for the last seven years has specialised in the genetics of ancient populations. She has experience of working with heavily degraded human and non-human samples. She has been continuously involved with public engagement activities, especially in collaboration with the Manchester Museum where she teaches science to students. Her research interests involve ancient DNA from archaeological remains for the purposes of disease identification, kinship analysis and population genetics. Her current research involves the evolution of schistosomiasis in ancient Egyptian populations.

Roger Forshaw was a dental surgeon in general practice before taking early retirement. He went on to study Egyptology at the University of Exeter and then at the University of Manchester where he obtained an MSc in Biomedical Egyptology and a PhD in Egyptology. He is at present an honorary lecturer in Biomedical Egyptology at Manchester and is involved with the new MSc online course in Biomedical Egyptology. His research interests include dental anthropology and dental care in the ancient world, healing practices in ancient Egypt, and a study of the Saite Period in ancient Egypt. His publications include *The Role of the Lector in Ancient Egyptian Society* (Archaeopress, 2014) and a number of academic papers on healing practices, dental care and dental health in ancient Egypt. His latest book, *Egypt of the Saite Pharaohs, 664–525 BC*, was published by Manchester University Press in 2019.

Sharon Fraser is currently a visiting scientist at the KNH Centre for Biomedical Egyptology at the University of Manchester. She completed an MEarthSci in 2003 followed by a PhD in 2007 at the University of Manchester, in which she used geochemical analysis for the prove-nancing of archaeological artefacts. Following her involvement in various research projects that combined geochemical analysis with archaeological questions, she now focuses on the use of organic analysis by gas chromatography mass spectrometry for investigating various types of archaeological artefacts.

Anthony Freemont is the Procter Professor of Pathology at the University of Manchester, a post he has held for 27 years. He is co-director of the KNH Centre for Biomedical Egyptology and the online MSc in Biomedical Egyptology. His major research interest is in the application of molecular pathology techniques to human tissue and body fluids to better understand the nature of disease. Working with colleagues he is now applying these techniques to mummified tissues to identify relationships between individuals and the patterns of disease in ancient Egypt.

Andrew Gize is an independent research consultant who specialises in organic geochemistry and petrography. In addition to several collaborative projects in ancient Egyptology with the KNH Centre for Biomedical Egyptology at the University of Manchester, his archaeology-based research has included studies of the geology of a late Minoan necropolis and the Stonehenge Bluestones.

Winifred Glover retired as Curator of World Cultures in the Ulster Museum, National Museums Northern Ireland, in 2011. She curated the Egyptian, Armada and Ethnographic collections, including Takabuti, for 38 years. A graduate of Queen's University Belfast, she was a member of the Irish Association of Professional Archaeologists, a founder member of the Museum Ethnographers Group, a member of the Historic Monuments Council for two terms and an alumnus of the Salzburg Seminar of 1987. She has published widely in archaeological and historical journals and written a book on the Ulster Museum's world-famous 'Girona' collection (2000) from the Spanish Armada of 1588. The mummy of Takabuti was a constant and intriguing companion during all her years working in the museum.

Robert Loynes obtained a PhD in Egyptology from the University of Manchester in 2014, after retiring from a career as an orthopaedic surgeon when he was awarded an MBE. Since then he has been involved in continuous research programmes using medical imaging and, in particular, CT scans to analyse mummification techniques and reveal pathology in ancient Egyptian mummies from sources including Egypt, Moscow, Italy, the USA and the UK. Following the publication of his thesis he has written chapters for several books and numerous articles on mummification in peer-reviewed journals. A regular speaker on the subject of mummification at international conferences, he also speaks to Egyptology societies in the UK and abroad and is in the process of compiling a metadata base of mummy CT scans to enable a more robust discourse on mummification techniques throughout the eras of Egyptian history.

Natalie McCreesh studied Takabuti as part of her PhD thesis at the University of Manchester, which she was awarded in 2010. Since then she has had a dedicated academic career, leaving her most recent position as senior lecturer in 2019 to pursue other interests. She is now CEO and founder of the creative consultancy Dogwood Lifestyle.

Jenefer Metcalfe is the centre manager for the KNH Centre for Biomedical Egyptology at the University of Manchester. Her research interests include the application of stable and radioactive isotopes to the study of human remains, especially Egyptian mummies, and the use of experimental models to study mummification techniques. She completed a PhD focusing on the application of radiocarbon dating to ancient Egyptian artefacts in 2006 at the University of Manchester and has previously worked as a research associate on several projects, including a reinvestigation of Manchester Mummy 1770 and a study of the human remains found during the Archaeological Survey of Nubia.

Gerry Millar is a former Northern Ireland GP of the Year. He works in the Southern Trust and is Macmillan GP Advisor in Cancer and Palliative Care for Northern Ireland and vice-chair of NI Hospice and Children's Hospice. He was awarded an MBE for services to healthcare and palliative care in 2013 and also honoured as a Macmillan UK Cancer Fellow. His fascination with the history of medicine began at the age of 12 and developed into research and lecturing on American Civil War medicine and, particularly, ancient Egyptian medicine and mummification. This interest, along with research into the pioneering Victorian Egyptologist Revd Dr Edward Hincks, led to his involvement in the Takabuti Project and a 2009 BBC Northern Ireland documentary. He is a Visiting Scholar in Queen's University Belfast and is currently investigating diseases in post-medieval Ireland.

Eileen Murphy is Professor of Archaeology and co-director of the Centre for Community Archaeology in the School of Natural and Built Environment, Queen's University Belfast. With a background in osteology, palaeopathology and funerary archaeology, her current research largely involves the study of ancient human skeletal remains and burial practices from Ireland and Russia. She is the author/editor of 11 books, and has published numerous articles in academic journals. She has been the editor of the international journal *Childhood in the Past* since its inception in 2008 and is also a member of the editorial board of the *European Journal of Archaeology*. She has had a long-standing fascination with Takabuti since visiting her in the Ulster Museum as a young child, and Takabuti was one of the main inspirations that resulted in her pursuing a career in archaeology.

Mark Regan is CEO of Kingsbridge Private Hospital in Belfast. Graduating from Ulster University in 1998 with a BSc (Hons) in Radiography, he worked in several medical imaging departments in Dublin and Antrim before leaving the NHS to embark on a career in the private sector. During this period he continued to lecture at the University of Ulster at both undergraduate and postgraduate levels. While the business aspects of healthcare have always been a draw for him, he has maintained his professional clinical registrations throughout this period, which ultimately allowed him to be part of the imaging team in the Takabuti Project. Having spent much of his early childhood in south Belfast, the attraction of a weekly visit to see the 'Egyptian Mummy' was the cornerstone of his fascination with Takabuti, one that has been revived in adulthood.

Paula Reimer is the director of the [14]CHRONO Centre for Climate, the Environment, and Chronology in Archaeology and Palaeoecology, School of Natural and Built Environment, Queen's University Belfast. Her research focuses on radiocarbon dating and calibration. From 2002 to 2020 she led the international IntCal Working Group which provides radiocarbon calibration curves used worldwide to put a calendar timescale on radiocarbon chronologies. She is also interested in radiocarbon offsets between marine or freshwater systems and the atmosphere. Her research outputs reflect the diverse, interdisciplinary nature of her work, which ranges from archaeological science to earth and ocean sciences.

Sarah Shrimpton is a postdoctoral research assistant in Face Lab at the School of Art and Design, Liverpool John Moores University. She has a background in fine art and, after graduating with an MSc in Forensic Art from the University of Dundee, she undertook a number of research positions that enabled her to focus on the recognition of altered facial images. This culminated in a PhD investigating the role of facial features in identity processing of composited faces. With a focus on the recognition of faces and facial depictions for forensic scenarios, her research centres around exploring various methods for the creation of facial depictions and synthetic faces through compositing, and how they are received, perceived and recognised by the public. She has carried out facial depiction work for forensic investigations both in the UK and internationally, and contributes to archaeological depiction work exhibited around the world.

John Taylor obtained his PhD from the University of Birmingham with a study of the stylistic evolution of Egyptian coffins of the Third Intermediate Period. Since 1988 he has worked in the Department of Egypt and Sudan at the British Museum, where his specialist interests have focused on funerary antiquities, mummification, bronze statuary and the history of Egyptology. He has participated in excavations at el-Amarna, Luxor and Hierakonpolis, and has curated a number of major exhibitions, including 'Journey through the Afterlife: Ancient Egyptian Book of the Dead' and 'Ancient Lives', which presented the results of an extensive study of mummies using CT scanning. He has published numerous books and articles, and is currently working on a catalogue of coffins of the 22nd–24th Dynasties in the British Museum.

David Tosh has been working as research co-ordinator for National Museums Northern Ireland since 2018, prior to which he worked in the field of conservation biology. When not learning about ancient Egypt and trying to borrow X-ray machines for projects on ancient mummies, he assists research across all areas of National Museums Northern Ireland's collections. Upon gaining a PhD in Ecotoxicology from Queen's University Belfast, he became interested in the distribution and population status of endangered species. He gained experience in working for the not-for-profit, government, university and private sectors in Indonesia, Ireland and the UK before hanging up his boots for a family and joining the museum. He continues to pursue an interest in the pine marten – but only at weekends.

Bart van Dongen is a reader in Organic Geochemistry at the University of Manchester. He obtained his MSc in Chemistry from the University of Leiden in 1997, completed his PhD research at the Royal Netherlands Institute for Sea Research in 2003 and, after performing postdoctoral research at the University of Bristol and Stockholm University, moved to Manchester in 2007 to accept a lectureship in the Department of Earth and Environmental Sciences. His current research focuses on the application of organic geochemical techniques to the study of biogeochemical processes, and he supervises the organic geochemical laboratories in the Williamson Research Centre. He has extensive experience with a large number of analytical techniques including GC and LC-MS, compound specific isotope and radiocarbon analyses, has published over 85 papers in peer-reviewed journals, is an associate editor for *Organic Geochemistry* and a board member of the European Association of Organic Geochemists.

Keith White is an honorary senior lecturer in Environmental Science and a member of the KNH Centre for Biomedical Egyptology at the University of Manchester. He was appointed to a lectureship at Manchester in 1981 and retired as senior lecturer in 2018. He has published nearly 80 peer-reviewed papers, several book chapters and numerous conference publications in environmental toxicology, aquatic pollution and water quality management. He was instrumental in initiating the water management approaches that were central to the success of the Salford Quays development in Greater Manchester and resulted in the launch of a highly successful environmental consultancy company. He has extensive experience with a number of analytical techniques including quantitative and quantitative trace element analysis, histology, light and electron microscopy and the use of aquatic biota as indicators of environmental stress. He is currently applying his environmental expertise to an examination of water provision in ancient Egypt.

Caroline Wilkinson is the director of Liverpool School of Art and Design, where she leads Face Lab, a research group at Liverpool John Moores University. She has a background in art and science and, after receiving her PhD from the University of Manchester, she led the Unit of Art in Medicine and received a NESTA Fellowship to develop a 3D computerised facial reconstruction system for use in forensic and archaeological depiction. She moved to Liverpool John Moores University from the University of Dundee, where she was Head of Human Identification in the award-winning Centre for Anatomy and Human Identification, and her high-profile work includes facial depictions of Richard III, J. S. Bach and Robert the Bruce. She is certified by the Royal Anthropological Institute (RAI) as a Forensic Anthropologist Level I (craniofacial specialism) and is an experienced practitioner, with facial depiction work exhibited in museums around the world.

Acknowledgements

We are grateful to the Friends of the Ulster Museum who generously funded many of the analyses that were undertaken during the 2018–19 studies of Takabuti. We are also grateful to J. H. Davidson, the Engaged Research Fund and the Culture and Society Research Cluster at Queen's University Belfast for kindly funding this book.

The staff of National Museums Northern Ireland provided stalwart support and facilitated the new research on Takabuti, and we are grateful to Kathryn Thomson, William Blair, Hannah Crowdy, David Tosh, Greer Ramsey, Joanne Lowe, Joanne Marshall and Fiona Baird.

The late Ian Dougan of Borderline Productions initiated the modern programme of research on Takabuti through his BBC Northern Ireland television programme *Show Me the Mummy: The Face of Takabuti*, and we are grateful to him for having the vision to bring the original team together and start this journey of discovery. We are also very appreciative to the 2008 production team for all their efforts to produce such a high-quality documentary, especially Tom Maguire and Joy Hines.

Some of the individuals from the earlier phase of the project are not contributors to this book, but we would like to acknowledge the contribution they made at that time – John Meneely, Queen's University Belfast, who laser-scanned Takabuti, and John Denton and Ken Wildsmith, then of the University of Manchester, who undertook endoscopy and initial histological investigations.

We are extremely grateful to Val Stevenson, the great granddaughter of William Darragh, who created the oil painting of Takabuti in 1880. Val contacted us after the press release about Takabuti in January 2020, and she kindly permitted us to include a copy of her great grandfather's painting in the book. The very talented Libby Mulqueeny, Queen's University Belfast, helped with maps and some of the images, as well as producing the watercolour paintings of the daily activities of a high-status ancient Egyptian woman, and we thank her for helping us to imagine Takabuti during life.

We are extremely grateful to Stephen Weir of the National Museums Northern Ireland Picture Library for providing us with numerous images from the archives. Campbell Price of the Manchester Museum, University of Manchester, kindly facilitated permission to use photographic images of objects in the museum collection. We also thank Catherine Giltrap of the Trinity College Dublin Art Collections for permitting us to include the portrait of the Revd Dr Edward Hincks. Thanks are also due to Barbara Vankets and Isabelle Artaud of the Réunion des Musées Nationaux Grand Palais, Angie McCarthy at the John Rylands Library, University of Manchester, and Paul McGuigan of Northern Star Pictures, for their help and advice with obtaining copyright permissions. We thank Stuart Cochrane, University of Manchester, for help with digital images. We are grateful to Professor Rick Schulting, University of Oxford, for permitting us to include a modified version of an image from his 1998 paper. We also thank Barrie Hartwell and Dr Svetlana Svyatko, Queen's University Belfast, Ray Williams, National Museums Northern Ireland, and Dr P. Rutherford, University of Manchester, for providing images included in the volume.

We would like to acknowledge PRONI, the Public Record Office of Northern Ireland, for their help with locating archive material about the Belfast Natural History and Philosophical Society. Dr Finbar McCormick, Queen's University Belfast, generously shared newspaper archive material. We are also grateful to Nicola McVeigh of Ulster Architectural Heritage for enabling us to gain access to the Old Museum Building. Many thanks are due to Kathryn McKavanagh, Queen's University Belfast, and Dr Bernadette Mulvenna FRCGP, Benburb, Co. Tyrone, for their support and interest in the project.

We are grateful to Anthony McKenna, Operations Manager, Kingsbridge Private Hospital, Belfast, for planning in relation to the X-ray analysis of Takabuti in the Ulster Museum in October 2018; Alan Calverd of Medical Physics, Radiation Consultancy Services, Twickenham, kindly provided advice around radiation physics and gained the necessary permissions from the Health and Safety Executive; and Ivar van Zijl, PACS Manager, Kingsbridge Private Hospital, performed the image reconstructions. Thanks are also due to Major Colin Roberts of the Crimean War Research Society, and Dr Christopher Gardner-Thorpe of the Worshipful Society of Apothecaries of London, for informative discussions; and to Dr Emyr Benbow, senior lecturer in pathology, University of Manchester, and consultant pathologist, Manchester Royal Infirmary, for insights concerning weapon trauma. Dr Jonathan Elias of the Akhmim Mummy

Studies Consortium kindly provided information on the use of magical poultices to induce healing. We thank Professor Anthony Whetton, University of Manchester, for his guidance in the principles and practice of proteomics, and Professor Kevin Cathcart, Emeritus Professor of Near Eastern Languages, University College Dublin, for sharing information on the Revd Dr Edward Hincks.

We are grateful to the staff of the ^{14}CHRONO Centre for Climate, the Environment and Chronology, Queen's University Belfast, for their help with radiocarbon dating, and especially Michelle Thompson, who prepared the hair samples for incremental isotopic analysis. We also appreciate the help provided by Keith Hall of Hall Analytical Ltd, Manchester, for advice on MSSV, and Steve Caldwell of the Williamson Research Centre, University of Manchester, for support with ESEM. We are grateful to Dr Peter Gasson of the Jodrell Laboratory, Royal Botanic Gardens, Kew, for confirming the presence of cedar wood in the packing material.

Finally we very much appreciate the unfailing support provided by Clare Litt of Liverpool University Press throughout the publication process, and the press's reviewer for their helpful suggestions. We also thank Carnegie Book Production for producing the book and Eileen O'Neill for preparing the index.

1

Takabuti:
The Historical Evidence

Introduction to the Takabuti Project
Rosalie David and Eileen Murphy

Takabuti, the subject of this book, was a young, upper-class woman who lived in Egypt during the 25th Dynasty (755–656 BC) of the Third Intermediate Period. She died when she was in her late 20s to early 30s; her body was mummified and she was most probably buried in the vicinity of the great religious centre of Thebes (modern Luxor) (Fig. 1). Her mummy and coffin were acquired by Thomas Greg, a wealthy young man from Holywood, Co. Down, when he visited Egypt in 1834, possibly as part of the 'Grand Tour', a common educational experience of the upper classes at that time. Mummified remains were prized souvenirs and many Egyptian tombs were robbed for the benefit of wealthy European travellers. Greg donated the mummy and coffin to the Belfast Natural History Society, and thus began Takabuti's connection with Northern Ireland. After much anticipation, she arrived on the island in the autumn of 1834. She was unwrapped on 27 January 1835 and an in-depth analysis was undertaken of her body and coffin by some of the greatest academic minds of the day. Since that time she has been a much-loved part of the story of Belfast and has been a highlight of the city's main museums over the years (see pp. 9–13). She was on show in the newly opened Belfast Municipal Museum and Art Gallery in 1929 and has been associated with this site, now referred to as the Ulster Museum, ever since. She inspired paintings and poetry when she was unwrapped (see Chapter 1, pp. 31–32) and afterwards; a notable example of this creativity is an oil painting of her created in 1880 (Fig. 2) by William Darragh, son of the longstanding curator of the Belfast Museum (from 1844–91) of the same name. More recently, a poem entitled 'The Mummy in the Ulster Museum' by Dehra Adams

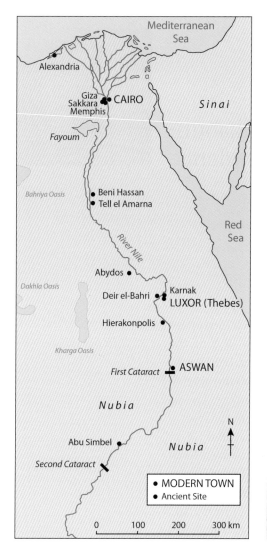

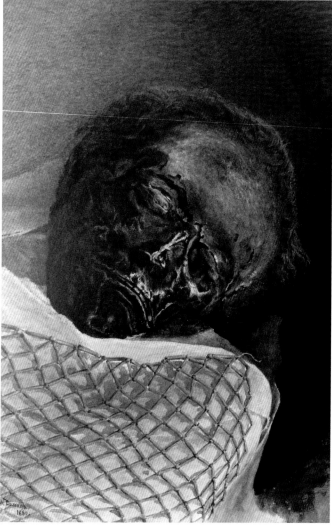

1 Map of Egypt.
(drawn by Libby Mulqueeny, Queen's University Belfast, after Partridge 2002: fig. 1)

2 Oil painting of Takabuti dating to 1880 by William Darragh, son of the then curator of the Belfast Museum (1844–91) of the same name.
(© Val Stevenson)

was published in the *Belfast News-Letter* on 20 January 1992, and Takabuti also made a brief appearance in the novel – *The Undead of Belfast* – by Tim Hodkinson published in 2017. Using the latest scientific techniques, the Takabuti Project has aimed to learn more about this woman's life, what happened to her body in the aftermath of her death, and the story of her existence as a mummified ancient Egyptian displayed in a museum environment.

'Mummy studies' undertaken on human remains from Egypt and many other countries have made great advances over the past 30 years. These usually involve an interdisciplinary approach, where a combination of historical evidence and scientific analysis provides a more complete picture of an individual's life and the society in which the person lived. However, this increased interest has raised questions about the ethics of research in this field, and the putting of Egyptian mummies on public display in museums (Day 2014). Opinions vary, and even when Dr Margaret Murray carried out her pioneering work in the early twentieth century, she faced some criticism. Her response was typically robust:

> To most people there are few ideas more repugnant than that of disturbing the dead. To open graves, to remove all the objects placed there by loving hands, and to unroll and investigate the bodies, seems to many minds not merely repulsive but bordering on sacrilege. And yet these same people would not hesitate to wear a scarab-ring taken off a dead man's hand … Their objections – their opinions even – are an offence to science. (Murray 1910: 7)

Murray goes on to explain how archaeology, including the investigation of ancient human remains, contributes to the universal acquisition of knowledge, and should therefore be regarded as valid and acceptable. In recent years, UK government reports have identified the overall contribution to knowledge and the modern world that the scientific investigation of human remains can make. A Department of Culture, Media and Sport report in 2005 (David 2008: 237–38) discusses a legal and ethical framework for the treatment of ancient human remains. It also recognises that, because of their unique status in museum and other collections, human remains require special attention, and it provides guidelines for their curation and sampling.

Ancient Egypt provides an unparalleled opportunity to study the early history of disease, medicine and pharmacology. Although the civilisation has left behind an abundance of written records and archaeological remains, biomedical and scientific studies provide a new and different dimension, often supplying information which is lacking or difficult to interpret in other sources. Unique geographical and environmental conditions in Egypt have ensured that human remains from all levels of society have been preserved. Mummification of the bodies has provided us with the opportunity to utilise a range of diagnostic scientific techniques on both skeletal remains and tissue samples. Unlike many other ancient societies, inscriptional source are available, and the contents of the medical papyri can be compared with palaeopathological findings.

In recent years, studies on Egyptian mummies have provided a historical context for research on 'modern' diseases, such as cancer, atherosclerosis and parasitic infestations, presenting an opportunity to ask how and why such conditions have developed in particular ways. Over the past 50 years, teams throughout the world have contributed to multidisciplinary investigations of mummies. These include major projects on royal and other mummies undertaken by Egyptian scientists

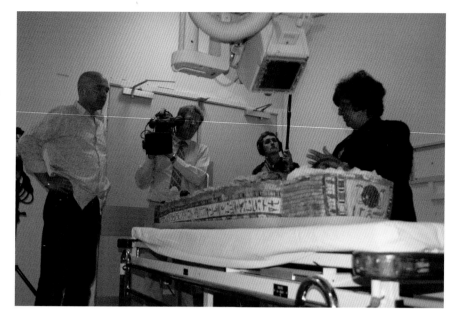

3 The film crew of the BBC Northern Ireland documentary *Show Me the Mummy: The Face of Takabuti*; from left Ian Dougan, Paul Littler and Christine Barker, discussing the scene to be shot with Professor Judith Adams.
(photograph courtesy of KNH Centre Archive, University of Manchester)

and archaeologists. It was within this context of seeking new knowledge about ancient Egypt, and making this available to both researchers and the wider public, that the Takabuti Project was initiated and developed in accordance with all recognised ethical standards and procedures.

The Takabuti Project has had two main phases of activity – one in 2007–09 and more recently in 2018–20. We will now provide an overview of these phases to set the scene for the chapters that follow. In autumn 2007 Ian Dougan, then a director and producer with Borderline Productions, who sadly passed away in 2018, initiated a chain of events that would realise his childhood wish to see the face of Takabuti restored (Fig. 3). With the closure of the Ulster Museum in 2006 for a period of

4 The title screen of the BBC Northern Ireland documentary *Show Me the Mummy: The Face of Takabuti.*
(© Ian Dougan, Borderline Productions)

major refurbishment, Ian seized the opportunity to instigate a programme of research on Takabuti which culminated in a one-hour documentary for BBC Northern Ireland – *Show Me the Mummy: The Face of Takabuti* – first aired in October 2009 (Fig. 4).

To obtain as much evidence as possible about Takabuti during life and in death, a team of experts was gathered from a range of organisations including National Museums Northern Ireland, Queen's University Belfast, the University of Manchester, the University of Cardiff and the University of Dundee. Many of these original researchers have also been involved in the more recent research which has enabled them to update their initial findings.

The 2007–09 research involved radiocarbon dating and stable isotope analysis undertaken in the [14]CHRONO Centre for Climate, the Environment and Chronology of Queen's University Belfast and led by Professor Paula Reimer. Dr Natalie McCreesh, in collaboration with Dr Andrew Gize, undertook a geochemical and morphological analysis of Takabuti's hair as part of her PhD research at the University of Manchester (McCreesh et al. 2011). Because only limited endoscopy on the mummy was permitted, John Denton and Ken Wildsmith of the University of Manchester were unable to recover any tissue samples, which could potentially have provided a wealth of information on her health status. However, the few samples that were retrieved confirmed that the original abdominal packing material largely comprised sawdust.

A major component of the first phase of research was imaging analysis, and this involved Takabuti being transported by boat and lorry to the Manchester Royal Infirmary, where radiography and CT scans were

5 A carefully packaged Takabuti being removed from a lorry by the driver, John Denton and Dr Gerry Millar, watched by Winifred Glover, Joanne Marshall and Professor Judith Adams, as she arrived at the Manchester Royal Infirmary where her mummy was X-rayed and CT-scanned. (photograph courtesy of Eileen Murphy, Queen's University Belfast)

taken of her under the guidance of the late Professor Judith Adams (Fig. 5). The images taken at that time enabled more recent imaging analysis to be undertaken in 2018–20. In the earlier study no cause of death was identified. It was concluded that her brain had not been extracted through the normal route via the ethmoid/sphenoid and that abdominal evisceration had occurred through the anus. A mysterious package located in the top left of her chest was interpreted as the bandaged remains of her heart. The heart was considered to be a vital element in allowing individual access to the afterlife and was needed for the final judgement when the soul of the deceased was weighed against the feather of truth before Osiris. This interpretation seemed feasible and was the accepted view until the recent examination of the images undertaken in 2018–20 by Dr Robert Loynes, which has resulted in a complete reinterpretation of the package.

One of the key aims of the 2007–09 phase of the project – and Ian Dougan's childhood wish – was to see how Takabuti would have looked when she was alive. A focal point of the research and the associated television programme was the production of a facial reconstruction based on Takabuti's skull which was made by Professor Caroline Wilkinson and Dr Sarah Shrimpton, then at the University of Dundee. When the Ulster Museum reopened its doors to the public in October 2009 the facial reconstruction was displayed alongside the mummy in a newly designed gallery for Egyptian antiquities.

In 2011 a summary of the research findings was published in the popular magazine *Ancient Egypt* (Murphy et al. 2011). The original team

6 The Egyptian Gallery in the Ulster Museum transformed into a laboratory on 8 October 2018. Dr Robert Loynes is preparing to take samples of packing material while Dr Konstantina Drosou looks on.
(photograph courtesy of Eileen Murphy, Queen's University Belfast)

7 Members of the Takabuti Project team at a one-day seminar entitled 'The "Belfast Mummy"' that was held at the University of Manchester on 25 January 2020. From left: Roger Forshaw, Eileen Murphy, Konstantina Drosou, Caroline Wilkinson, Robert Loynes, Anthony Freemont, Keith White, David Tosh, Sarah Shrimpton and Rosalie David. (photograph courtesy of Konstantina Drosou, University of Manchester)

also came together that year to share their findings at a session devoted to Takabuti held at the World Mummy Congress in San Diego, California. Although attempts to publish the findings as a book foundered at that time, this turned out to be advantageous, since the current project has benefited from substantial developments in techniques now available to researchers in this field.

In 2018 the second phase of the Takabuti Project commenced with funding support generously provided by the Friends of the Ulster Museum. With the support of the National Museums Northern Ireland staff, particularly William Blair, Hannah Crowdy and Dr Greer Ramsey, and coordinated by Dr David Tosh, research co-ordinator for National Museums Northern Ireland, some members of the original team were reunited, while new members joined. The remit of the work was very clear – to tie up some of the loose ends from the original programme of work. What was the nature of the mysterious package in Takabuti's chest? Did her tissues contain any evidence of disease? What was her cause of death? Could information be found about her ancestry? Members of the team assembled in the Ulster Museum on 8 October 2018 for an intensive day of sampling. The Egyptian Gallery was turned into a makeshift laboratory and Takabuti was removed from her glass case (Fig. 6). Mark Regan of Kingsbridge Private Hospital set up an X-ray C-arm image intensifier over her coffin, while Dr Robert Loynes gently used a bone biopsy needle to take tiny samples of packing material, as well as bone and muscle tissue, from within her torso and right thigh. Sampling for DNA from these samples required all those involved to don full forensic suits. A new sample of hair was taken for incremental isotopic analysis, while a sample of resin was taken from the collar around her neck.

Over the following year the researchers processed their samples and the new results were gradually revealed. This culminated in a one-day seminar entitled 'The "Belfast Mummy"' that was held at the University of Manchester on 25 January 2020, during which many of the researchers involved in both phases of the project came together to share their findings (Fig. 7). Another milestone in the project occurred two days later on 27 January – the 185th anniversary of Takabuti's unwrapping – when some of the exciting new results were revealed to the public and the new display panels in her gallery were launched. There was much media interest in the discovery that, contrary to the view held for the previous 185 years, Takabuti had not had a peaceful end but rather had died at the hands of another.

We hope you will enjoy this volume, which brings together the results of the extensive historical and scientific research that has been undertaken on Takabuti. She holds a special place in the hearts of the people of Northern Ireland, and the volume is intended to show her the utmost respect by keeping her name alive – a key component of ancient Egyptian rituals to guarantee success in the afterlife.

References

David, R. (ed.) 2008. *Egyptian Mummies and Modern Science*. Cambridge: Cambridge University Press.

Day, J. 2014. 'Thinking makes it so': reflections on the ethics of displaying Egyptian mummies. *Papers on Anthropology* 23, 29–44.

McCreesh, N. C., Gize, A. P. and David, A. R. 2011. Ancient Egyptian 'hair gel': new insight into ancient Egyptian mummification procedures through chemical analysis. *Journal of Archaeological Science* 38, 3432–34.

Murphy, E., David, R. and Glover, W. 2011. Takabuti: a twenty-fifth dynasty Egyptian lady. *Ancient Egypt*, 11(5), 22–27.

Murray, M. A. 1910. *The Tomb of Two Brothers*. Manchester: Sherratt & Hughes.

Partridge, R. B. 2002. *Fighting Pharaohs: Weapons and Warfare in Ancient Egypt*. Manchester: Peartree Publishing.

Takabuti and the Museums of Belfast

Eileen Murphy

Takabuti has found a home in three different institutions since her arrival in Belfast in 1834, and this section provides an overview of her story as part of a museum collection since that time. In addition to a detailed account of Takabuti's unwrapping, the *Belfast News-Letter* contained an advertisement on 30 January 1835 that informed the public that her mummy would be displayed unwrapped for four days. After this time the bandages were to be replaced, with the exception of those at the head and feet, and the mummy was to remain on display in the Belfast Museum on College Square North (Fig. 1). Takabuti's wrappings have remained like this to the present day, and, for much of her time in the Belfast Museum, she appears to have been displayed in the room in which she was unwrapped.

From 1 May 1837 the museum was opened to the public for six days each week and the admission fee was reduced to threepence for 'mechanics' and children and sixpence for everyone else (Nesbitt 1979: 13). The Belfast Museum was a popular venue for the citizens of Belfast, and between 1845 and 1910, the Society promoted the museum as a special attraction on Easter Monday, which was one of the main holidays for the city's working classes (Fig. 2). The entry fee for that day was fixed at twopence for adults and one penny for children. Large numbers of visitors attended the museum in the morning before going to the Botanic Gardens for a balloon ascent in the afternoon. Takabuti was one of the greatest attractions for the Easter Monday crowds, 'which they seemed never tired of inspecting' (Deane 1924: 16).

Egyptian Mummy.

THE EGYPTIAN MUMMY, unrolled in the BELFAST MUSEUM on TUESDAY last. may be seen, in its present state, To-morrow, SATURDAY the 31st inst. and on MONDAY the 2d, WEDNESDAY the 4th, and FRIDAY the 6th of February. The *Bandages will then be replaced, with the exception of those on the Head and Feet; and the Mummy will remain for Exhibition in the Large Room in which the Collection is at present arranged.

Admittance to Non-Subscribers, One Shilling.

Signed,

R. S. McADAM,
JAS. D. MARSHALL, M.D. } *Secretaries.*

Friday, 30th Jan. 1835.

1 Announcement to the public of the first opportunity to see Takabuti, published in the *Belfast News-Letter* on 30 March 1835. (PRONI D3263.E.1)

2 Poster advertising the Belfast Museum as an attraction on Easter Monday 1907, with a prominent reference to Takabuti.
(© National Museums NI, Collection Ulster Museum)

Over the succeeding decades the Belfast Museum underwent changes and development, most notably an expansion of the premises in 1880 to accommodate the growing collections. In 1899 a visitor's guide to the museum entitled *Notes on Some of the More Interesting Objects in the Belfast Museum* was produced by Samuel Alexander Stewart, curator of the museum 1891–1907, which underwent several editions. In the 1904 edition it is recorded that Takabuti and the museum's other Egyptian antiquities were on display in the Ethnography Room, located to the right of the entrance (PRONI D2194/49/12), indicating that she had been moved from the upper room where she had been unwrapped.

At the end of the nineteenth century there was a strong feeling in Belfast that the city authorities should erect a major museum that would reflect the growth of the city. The Belfast Free Public Library was opened on Royal Avenue on 13 October 1888, and rebranded as the Belfast Free Public Library Art Gallery and Museum on 16 July 1890. Much of the new museum's early archaeo-logical and natural history collections stemmed from a donation from Canon John Grainger in 1891, and were displayed in what was referred to as the 'Grainger Room'. On 27 July 1910 the Belfast Natural History and Philosophical Society gifted their collections to the city (Deane 1924: 14; Nesbitt 1979: 23). Many of the Belfast Museum's collections remained stored in the College Square North building, however, and it was not fully cleared until 31 October 1928. Takabuti appears to have been moved to the Royal Avenue building prior to this time, however, and two photographs taken by A. R. Hogg indicate that she was certainly curated in this building by 1917. One of the photos was taken that year in the Grainger Room in the aftermath of a lecture on weeds by the museum's curator Arthur Deane. It clearly shows the upper part of Takabuti's sarcophagus in a display case in the background (Fig. 3). The second photo is of uncertain date but it shows Takabuti herself in the new museum (Fig. 4). Footage of James Boyce (b. 1909) as part of the BBC *Roving Reporter* series from around 1960 includes his reminiscences of visiting the museum as a young child, and his comments suggest that both Takabuti and her case were displayed in the Grainger Room.[1]

As early as 1909 the Corporation of the City of Belfast began to formu-late plans for a purpose-built museum, but progress was slow and the First

1 https://www.bbc.co.uk/archive/roving-reporter--belfast-old-museum/zr9m92p (last accessed 21 September 2020).

3 Photograph taken in the aftermath of Mr Deane's lecture on weeds in the Belfast Free Public Library Art Gallery and Museum in 1917 by A. R. Hogg. The top of Takabuti's sarcophagus can be clearly seen in the case in the background.
(© National Museums NI, Collection Ulster Museum)

World War negatively impacted upon the project. The Belfast Municipal Museum and Art Gallery was finally opened in 1929 on the Botanic Gardens site, near the Stranmillis Road, and today still forms part of the Ulster Museum (renamed 1 April 1962) (Fig. 5). Takabuti would have made the move to the Stranmillis site during 1928 when the Royal Avenue building was cleared of its museum collections, and she has been curated in this location since that time.

A major extension of the Ulster Museum commenced in 1966, and in 1969 all but the ground floor of the museum was closed to the public (Nesbitt 1979: 51–53). During this time Takabuti was moved to the entrance hall – a newspaper account of the day states that she was one of the most popular items in the museum, visited by around 100,000 people each year. It notes that at one stage she had to move temporarily within the Antiquities Gallery because a track had been worn around her case and the tiles had to be repaired (Ballantyne 1970). When the extended museum opened to the public in 1971 Takabuti was placed in the newly designed Non-Irish Antiquities Gallery. She was displayed at various locations around this large gallery until in 1987 her curator, Winifred Glover, secured the room in which she is currently displayed as an Ancient Civilisations Gallery.

When the museum was closed in October 2006 to undergo a period of refurbishment (Fig. 6) Takabuti underwent scientific study, including a brief foray to Manchester in 2008 as part of the BBC Northern Ireland *Show me the Mummy: The Face of Takabuti* television production (see Chapter 1, pp. 4–5). When the museum reopened in October 2009 Takabuti's case was reinstated in the centre

of what then became referred to as the Egyptian Gallery. The panels in her room
were updated in January 2020 to include key findings derived from the second
phase of the Takabuti Project relating to how she had been mummified and how
she had died (Fig. 7). No doubt Takabuti's museum story will not end there and
her modern resting place will see further changes over the years, when we are
all long gone.

6 Takabuti in the Non-Irish Antiquities Gallery, where she was located from 1971 following extension of the Ulster Museum.
(© National Museums NI, Collection Ulster Museum)

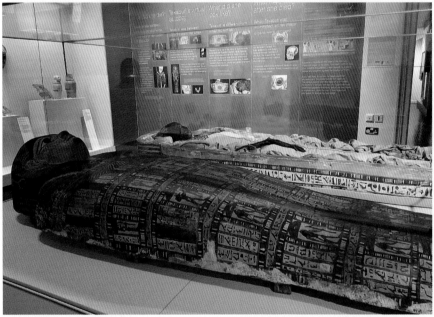

7 Takabuti in the Egyptian Gallery following the updating of the information panels in January 2020.
(photograph courtesy of Ray Williams, National Museums NI)

References

Ballantyne, N. 1970. Teenager from the tombs still top of the pops. *News Letter*, 10 April.

Deane, A. (ed.) 1924. *The Belfast Natural History and Philosophical Society. Centenary Volume, 1821–1921*. Belfast: Belfast Natural History and Philosophical Society.

Nesbitt, N. 1979. *A Museum in Belfast: A History of the Ulster Museum and its Predecessors*. Belfast: Ulster Museum.

Life and Death in Egypt during the 25th Dynasty
Rosalie David

The Historical Context

A detailed study of this mummy and coffin has provided information about the owner's life and death. On the basis of the stylistic criteria and inscriptions, the coffin has been dated to the 25th Dynasty (c. 755–656 BC) (see p. 24). According to the hieroglyphs, the coffin belonged to a woman of high status named Takabuti, and scientific evidence strongly suggests that the mummy belonged with the coffin (see Chapter 2, pp. 44–47). Although the provenance of the mummy and coffin are unknown, there are strong indications that Takabuti lived, died and was buried in the vicinity of the great religious centre of Thebes (modern Luxor). Her mummy and coffin were purchased in Luxor (see Chapter 1, p. 28), and her father, described in the inscriptions as a priest of Amun, probably served in the god's temple at Thebes (Fig. 1).

1 The Great Hypostyle Hall, Temple of Amun at Karnak, Thebes, showing decorated columns with plant-form capitals. Coloured lithograph by Louis Haghe after David Roberts, 1846.
(Creative Commons Attribution International licence (CC BY 4.0), https://commons.wikimedia.org/wiki/File:Decorated_pillars_of_the_temple_at_Karnac,_Thebes,_Egypt._Co_Wellcome_V0049316.jpg)

Takabuti lived at a time of great political uncertainty and upheaval (Kitchen 1996). In the eighth century BC a new power emerged in Kush, a region situated beyond Egypt's southern border and modern northern Sudan (Welsby 1996). Here, the Kushite rulers established their capital at Napata. Regarding themselves as the heirs of the Egyptian kings who had ruled this area in the 18th Dynasty (c. 1569–1315 BC), they adopted aspects of Egyptian civilisation, building pyramids for royal burials (Fig. 2), and promoting a local form of the Egyptian god Amun. They expanded and refurbished his temple at Gebel Barkal (Napata) which had fallen into disrepair after Egypt lost control of the area during the 20th Dynasty (1200–1081 BC).

2 The pyramids at Gebel Barkal (Napata) in Kush (the Sudan). From Cailliaud's *Voyage à Méroé au Fleuve Blanc* (1823). (© University of Manchester)

Next, the Kushite rulers moved north to conquer Egypt. Kashta occupied Aswan and may have tried to take Thebes. His successor, Piye (Piankhy), established a military base in southern Egypt, but when Tefnakht, a local ruler of Sais in the western Delta, began to seize control of provinces in northern and middle Egypt, Piye retaliated by leading a major military campaign northwards to Memphis (c. 728 BC). Tefnakht fled back to Sais, but all the other Delta princes submitted to Piye, who subsequently returned to Napata. Kushite control of Egypt was finally achieved when Shabaka (Piye's brother and successor) invaded the country and took Memphis. Subsequently establishing himself as the first king of the 25th Dynasty, Shabaka briefly reversed Egypt's long-standing colonisation of its southern neighbour (Fig. 3).

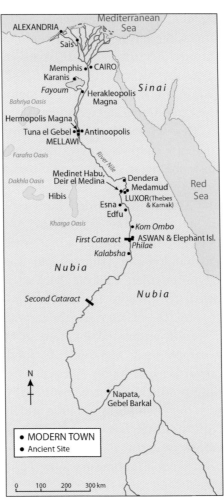

3 Map of Egypt and Nubia. (drawn by Libby Mulqueeny, Queen's University Belfast, after Partridge 2002: fig. 391)

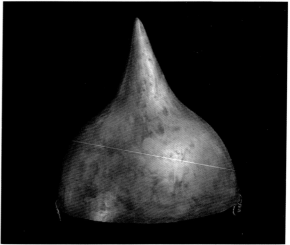

4 Courtyard in the Temple of Amun at Karnak, Thebes. Taharka's name is inscribed on the remaining column of the colonnade built during his reign.
(photograph courtesy of Rosalie David, University of Manchester)

5 Assyrian helmet from Thebes, Egypt, 25th Dynasty (c. 775–665 BC), Manchester Museum.
(© Manchester Museum, University of Manchester)

A period of significant cultural recovery now replaced the decline of the final years of the Third Intermediate Period (1081–711 BC). Religious building programmes flourished and, despite this dynasty's foreign origin, there is no evidence that non-Egyptian features were introduced into architecture or artistic styles. Indeed, examples of archaism (copying styles prevalent in the Old [c. 2687–c. 2191 BC] and Middle Kingdoms [2061–1760 BC]) are found in many tombs, and the temples retained all their traditional elements (Fig. 4).

Meanwhile, the Assyrians emerged in their northern homeland (modern Iraq) as a new, powerful adversary – a formidable military force characterised by compulsory military service and advanced weaponry (Kuhrt 2020) (see pp. 96–99). At first, relations between Egypt and Assyria were cordial, but Egypt's policy of assisting its client-states in Syria/Palestine against the Assyrians soon led to confrontations between the Egyptian kings and the Assyrian rulers Sennacherib, Esarhaddon and Ashurbanipal. The first invasion in 671 BC drove the Egyptian ruler, Taharka, back to Kush, but he subsequently returned briefly to intrigue against the pro-Assyrian local officials installed to govern the country. Esarhaddon's death en route to Egypt thwarted a second attempted invasion in 669 BC. His son Ashurbanipal sent a campaign in 668–667 BC, forcing Taharka to flee to Thebes and onwards to Kush (Fig. 5). Egypt was now incorporated into the Assyrian Empire, and henceforth governed by local pro-Assyrian rulers. However, ongoing attempts by Taharka and his successor, Tanutamun, to intrigue with these officials brought swift revenge from Assyria. Ashurbanipal's troops returned in 664/663 BC to attack Memphis and sack Thebes, prompting Tanutamun's final flight to Kush, which marked the end of the 25th Dynasty (Fig. 6).

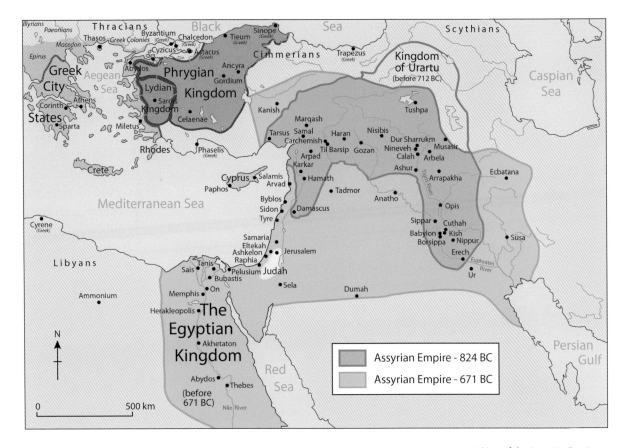

6 Map of the Assyrian Empire.
(drawn by Libby Mulqueeny, Queen's University Belfast)

Takabuti's Family Background

We can only speculate about the circumstances of Takabuti's life and death against this background of political intrigue and widespread military violence. However, the coffin inscriptions provide some reliable information about her personal circumstances. She carried the titles 'Lady of the House' and 'Noblewoman' (see pp. 26–27) and her deceased parents are named as Nespare, a priest of the god Amun, and his wife, Tasenirit.

From earliest times, ancient Egyptian society contained people from a mixture of ethnic backgrounds. They included merchants, traders, craftsworkers and prisoners-of-war. From 1000 BC onwards, successive conquests of Egypt by Kushites, Assyrians, Persians, Greeks and Romans further increased this genetic diversity. Takabuti's own ancestry – as demonstrated by DNA sequencing and studies on her hair – exemplifies the genetic diversity of her society (see Chapter 2, pp. 52–57 and p. 61).

As a priest's daughter, Takabuti would have enjoyed a privileged childhood and upbringing. Priests were allowed to marry and live with their families in the community, but were expected to reside within the temple precinct while undertaking temple duties. The Temple of Amun at

Karnak (where Nespare probably served) was greatly enhanced by royal donations of booty from foreign conquests throughout the New Kingdom (c. 1569–1081 BC). From the 18th Dynasty (c. 1569–1315 BC), its priesthood achieved unrivalled status and unprecedented religious, political and economic power (Fig. 7).

The functions of state and religion had been closely integrated from earliest times. Traditionally, the priesthood was held as a secondary profession: a rota involved each priest in one month's temple service, performed three times annually. For the remainder of the time, priests worked in the community and, being literate, many served as doctors, lawyers or scribes. Throughout the Old and Middle Kingdoms, temples were run by this lay clergy, mainly drawn from local elite families. By the New Kingdom, however, while the priesthood still largely functioned on a part-time basis, a permanent class of clergy had been introduced to meet the growing demands of larger temples. This arrangement was still in place in the 25th Dynasty.

As the 'House of the God', each temple provided a residence for a particular deity, but was never used for congregational worship. The prime role of priests, who had no pastoral duties, was to present food and other offerings to the temple gods – a daily duty delegated from the king who in theory acted as the sole priest in every temple (David 2002). Although many priests doubtless upheld society's ethical and moral standards, personal spirituality or vocation were not prerequisite. Individuals primarily sought these often hereditary offices to acquire wealth, privilege and, increasingly, political and economic power.

Temple employees included a wide range of people. The Temple of Amun at Karnak was led by a high priest ('First Prophet of Amun'), assisted by the 'Fathers of the God' ('Second, Third and Fourth Prophets

7 Capitals in the Temple of Amun at Karnak, Thebes, showing the remains of a stone grid (clerestory lighting) inserted between the roof and the walls. This provided the main illumination for the temple.
(photograph courtesy of Rosalie David, University of Manchester)

of Amun'). These senior priests undertook liturgical duties and performed the daily rituals for the gods, since they alone had regular access to the divine images within the sanctuary. Each ordinary priest was known as a 'Servant of the God'; they assisted with other religious ceremonies, and supervised the renovation, decoration and cleaning of the temple. Some clergy also taught their specialisms in medicine and science in temples designated as medical and educational centres. A large supporting staff produced food and other offerings for the gods.

Living in the 25th Dynasty

On reaching adulthood, Takabuti would have taken her place in elite society. According to traditional practice, her coffin inscriptions record the names of her parents but not her spouse. However, the title 'Lady of the House' indicates that she was a married woman of high status who supervised a substantial household.

In the 25th Dynasty, Thebes functioned as a major political, economic and religious centre. Here, as elsewhere, urban populations lived either in densely occupied townhouses or locally in the countryside. Unlike the stone-built pyramids, tombs and temples, domestic buildings were constructed of perishable materials, so relatively few examples of houses have survived. However, tomb wall-scenes and tomb models provide further information about their design and construction.

Many high-status families lived in spacious, two-storeyed country villas, and Takabuti and her family may have owned such a property. Design features kept the house cool throughout the summer. A central courtyard provided family space away from the heat and dust, and there were also reception areas for entertaining visitors, women's quarters, washing and bathing rooms, a kitchen, as well as cellars and granaries. Elite homes were comfortably, even luxuriously, decorated and furnished. Country houses were generally surrounded by formal gardens featuring flowering plants and shrubs, and some were at the core of sizeable estates which employed many household and outdoor servants (Fig. 8). The overall management of the largest estates was entrusted to a head steward. As 'Lady of the House', Takabuti would have supervised the domestic servants. If she had children (the mummy provides no confirmatory evidence of this), she would have been responsible for their early upbringing and education.

Dress styles doubtless evolved over the millennia, but surviving evidence does not provide much information about Takabuti's own attire. Surviving examples of clothing and jewellery are generally representative of periods before or after the 25th Dynasty, while religious conservatism ensured that tomb wall-scenes, regardless of their date, depicted the elite wearing formal, traditional clothing: linen garments, plant-fibre sandals, elaborate wigs and traditional jewellery. Evidence from art representations and many mummies shows that most people traditionally shaved their heads and wore wigs. It is therefore unusual that Takabuti retained her own hair, and it seems unlikely that she would have covered her elaborate hairstyle with a wig (see Chapter 2, pp. 62–64). The Egyptians' preoccupation with personal hygiene, beauty care, and cosmetics is exemplified by Takabuti's manicured nails and

8 Artist's impression of Takabuti in the garden of her home in Thebes.
(Libby Mulqueeny, Queen's University Belfast)

9 Artist's impression of Takabuti (seated on left) and members of her household preparing for a party.
(Libby Mulqueeny, Queen's University Belfast)

hairstyle, set into neat artificial curls and coated with a 'hair-gel' (see Chapter 2, pp. 61–63). She was doubtless the proud owner of an extensive toilette and wide range of cosmetics (Fig. 9).

Diet and Health

In childhood, Takabuti would have enjoyed the rich and varied food that her father brought home from the temple as his daily stipend – his share of the offerings that reverted from the gods' altars. As an adult, Takabuti's mixed diet conformed to the usual eating habits (see Chapter 3, pp. 88–90). It would have included a wide variety of fruit, vegetables, and foods such as bread and cereals that were produced from wheat and barley. Freshwater fish would have been available, and also meat. This was only included in most people's diet during certain religious festivals, but was more widely available for the elite. Excessive tooth wear, predominantly on the biting surfaces of the teeth, was a common health problem. Examination of bread samples has shown the cause to be the inclusion of husks of corn and mineral particles from windblown sand and the quern stones used to grind the cereal. Unusually, Takabuti's teeth and gums were trouble-free (see Chapter 3, pp. 71–74). Scientific studies to identify disease in mummies have recently entered a new and exciting phase (see Chapter 3, pp. 75–82). Environmentally induced diseases including parasitic infestations and sand pneumoconiosis are prevalent among previously reported conditions. Takabuti's mummy is an exception. Although restricted tissue sampling prevented immunological or extensive histological studies, imaging

10 The mummified body of Takabuti. The Egyptians usually shaved their heads, so Takabuti's elaborate hairstyle is unusual.
(photograph courtesy of Rosalie David, University of Manchester)

analysis (see Chapter 3, pp. 65–66) and dental investigation have shown that she was a young, healthy woman. Usually, the cause of death cannot be identified in mummies but, in this instance, research has revealed that Takabuti met a violent and untimely end (see Chapter 4, pp. 91–95).

Funerary Beliefs and Customs

The basic aim of Egyptian mummification was to preserve the body so that it could be recognised by the deceased owner's spirit, which was thought to enter the mummy and absorb the essence of food offerings placed nearby in the tomb. The earliest elite and non-elite graves were shallow depressions in the sand – ideal environmental conditions to desiccate and preserve the bodies. However, the situation changed with the introduction of brick-built tombs for elite burials. Bodies now rapidly deteriorated, and other ways of preserving the dead had to be found. Various experiments led to 'intentional mummification' which involved the evisceration of the body followed by dehydration of the tissues by means of natron, a naturally occurring salt compound.

Takabuti's body was mummified with great care (Fig. 10). Imaging analysis has revealed unusual features about the procedure (see Chapter 4, pp. 100–106), and new information from other studies increases knowledge about the substances and materials used to pack and preserve the body (see Chapter 4, pp. 107–10). The mummy would have been placed inside its own inscribed coffin or nest of coffins (see pp. 24–27). These provided physical protection and a spiritual locus to which the deceased's spirit could return. Over the millennia, the West Bank – a desolate area across the river from Thebes – was used extensively as a burial site for the inhabitants of Thebes. Although the provenance of Takabuti's mummy and coffin are unknown, and her tomb cannot be identified, she was probably buried somewhere in this region. When the funerary entourage reached the tomb, the mourners would have joined in a final meal, while priests performed special rites to ensure the deceased's safe passage to the afterlife.

Access to the afterlife was dependent on the correct performance of the burial procedures and rituals, and a successful outcome at the Day of Judgement. By reciting 42 statements from the 'Negative Confession' before a divine tribunal, the deceased denied any breach of Egypt's moral code and hoped to be judged worthy of eternal life.

Egyptians believed that non-royals spent the afterlife in an underworld kingdom ruled by the god Osiris. Situated below the western horizon, this was a mirror-image of Egypt, but there was no suffering, and its inhabitants enjoyed eternal springtime, freedom from disease and death, abundant food and drink, and reunion with their families and pets. Everyone also retained or regained their youth, and the elite expected to keep their wealth and status. Takabuti's tomb-assemblage doubtless included items to enhance her personal comfort and well-being in this eternal kingdom.

References

David, R. 2002. *Religion and Magic in Ancient Egypt*. Harmondsworth: Penguin.

Kitchen, K. A. 1996. *The Third Intermediate Period in Egypt (1100–650 BC)*. 2nd rev. edn. Warminster: Aris & Phillips.

Kuhrt, A. 2020. *The Ancient Near East c. 3000–330 BC*. Vol. 2 (Kindle edition). London: Routledge.

Partridge, R. B. 2002. *Fighting Pharaohs: Weapons and Warfare in Ancient Egypt*. Manchester: Peartree Publishing.

Welsby, D. A. 1996. *The Kingdom of Kush: The Napatan and Meroitic Empires*. London: Trustees of the British Museum.

The Coffin of Takabuti

John Taylor

The earliest Egyptian coffins were rectangular chests, but these were superseded at the beginning of the New Kingdom by cases shaped like a human body. Every aspect of the coffin's form and decoration was imbued with symbolic meaning and magical potency, equipping it to play a significant role in transmitting the deceased to eternal life. The mummiform coffin was both a divine image and a manifestation of sacred space, in which the mysteries of rebirth would take place.

Based on the stylistic criteria of Takabuti's coffin, it can be firmly dated to the 25th Dynasty (Aston 2009; Taylor 2003). It represents her in fully three-dimensional form like a statue, with a back-pillar, and a pedestal supporting her feet (Fig. 1). The limbs are concealed as if by a shroud, recalling the image of Osiris, or perhaps more specifically the threefold god Ptah-Sokar-Osiris, with whom the deceased was closely identified in this period. The coffin thus represents Takabuti as a mortal who has passed through the rites of embalming and is assimilated with the god, a transformation that would bring regeneration. Every dead person became 'an Osiris', but the association of a deceased female with a masculine deity created an ideological anomaly. Over time, the Egyptians sought to resolve this seeming contradiction in different ways – ultimately by identifying deceased women with Hathor, the goddess who protected the dead and acted as a feminine counterpart of Osiris in this role (Fig. 2). Although this connection was not usually made explicit in a coffin's texts until a later date, Takabuti's link with Hathor is probably alluded to visually by her winged headdress (Taylor 2017), an attribute of important goddesses.

The face mask of the coffin is a generic image, produced according to standard models by craftsmen who may never have seen the occupant when living (Fig. 3). Hence neither the mask nor the image of Takabuti on the breast of the coffin give any clue to her physical appearance, hair colour, age at death or preferred manner of dress and personal adornment. She is represented in an ideal state of youth and beauty, as she wished to exist for eternity.

Like the face on the coffin lid, the many inscriptions and small images on the surface are elements of a standardised pattern of decoration. Nevertheless, they were believed to enshrine magical potential to evoke sacred environments and ritual contexts. The entire cosmos in which the dead woman would exist is referenced by the

1 The coffin and mummy of Takabuti.
(© National Museums NI, Collection Ulster Museum)

image of the goddess Nut spreading her wings over the breast. She is simultaneously the divine mother and the personification of the heavens. A solar disc on the top of the head (Fig. 4) is paired with a painting beneath the feet showing the Apis bull carrying the mummy of the deceased towards the tomb (Fig. 5), images which reference the cardinal points of east and west, embedding Takabuti within a perpetual cycle of death and rebirth.

Much of the front of the coffin lid is occupied by figures of deities, each in a shrine and accompanied by inscriptions which purport to be the speeches of the divine beings depicted: these include the Four Sons of Horus, two forms of the embalmer god Anubis, and the protective eyes of Horus. Completed by a winged figure of Isis over the feet, this framework of divine powers is a schematic allusion to the place of mummification, in which the corpse was mummified and where, during the night before the burial, it was supposed to lie on a bier, surrounded

2 Hathor-headed capital, once part of a column in the Temple of Denderah, Graeco-Roman Period.
(photograph courtesy of Keith White, University of Manchester)

3 Face of the coffin of Takabuti showing stylised image of the owner.
(© National Museums NI, Collection Ulster Museum)

4 Solar disc painted on the top end of Takabuti's coffin.
(© National Museums NI, Collection Ulster Museum)

5 Painted image on the base of Takabuti's coffin, showing the Apis bull carrying the owner's mummy towards the tomb.
(© National Museums NI, Collection Ulster Museum)

6 Painted figure of a protective god on Takabuti's coffin. Takabuti's name is written in the horizontal bands of hieroglyphs above and below this figure, and in the vertical panel to the right.
(© National Museums NI, Collection Ulster Museum)

by deities who formed a cordon of protection against the hostile forces of Seth, the murderer of Osiris and enemy of the deceased.

Although the protective deities are conceived as standing around the body as it lay recumbent, they, like all of the decoration, are oriented vertically (Fig. 6). In this way they would be seen to full effect on the day of burial, when the mummy in its coffin was placed upright at the entrance to the tomb – a symbolic resurrection – so that the Opening of the Mouth ritual could be performed to reanimate the dead person. The inscription in the centre of the lid is a formula which invokes the sun god Re-Horakhty to provide 'a good burial in the necropolis in the desert on the West of Thebes for the ka [spirit] of the Osiris, the Lady of the House Takabuti'. The request for a 'good burial' occurs in some of the oldest mortuary literature from Egypt and was reintroduced in the 25th Dynasty, a time characterised by the revival of traditions from the great ages of the past. Directly above this inscription is an image of the deceased adoring Osiris and Isis, following the weighing of her heart in a balance, a procedure by which the gods judged a person's worthiness to receive eternal life. This vindication of the deceased was an important stage between burial and ascent to the sky as a transfigured spirit, and was nearly always referenced on the coffin.

Takabuti's coffin, then, manifests her exalted status after death, but it also reflects her rank in ancient Egyptian society during her life. Only members of the elite could afford painted coffins; the decoration followed established patterns, subject to variation according to the person's status (Taylor 2018). As daughter of a minor priest of Amun, Takabuti's place was somewhere in the middle of the elite group, and this is reflected in the adornment of her coffin. While the prominent display of hieroglyphic texts on the surface was itself a status symbol, they consist mainly of short formulaic speeches of gods, which were doubtless within the competence of most scribes. There are no specific spells from the *Book of the Dead* or the *Pyramid Texts* which would have required a higher level of scribal expertise and consequently would have incurred greater expense. Such texts are generally associated with the burials of more senior priests and officials and their families. Nevertheless, Takabuti was well provided for at her death; her surviving coffin would have been the innermost container of a 'nest', comprising two or three coffins one inside the other, to provide both physical and symbolic security on her journey to eternity.

References

Aston, D. A. 2009. *Burial Assemblages of Dynasty 21–25. Chronology – Typology – Developments*. Österreichische Akademie der Wissenschaften. Denkschriften der Gesamtakademie 54. Vienna: Verlag der Osterreichischen Akademie der Wissenschaften.

Taylor, J. H. 2003. Theban coffins from the Twenty-second to the Twenty-sixth Dynasty: dating and synthesis of development. In N. Strudwick and J. H. Taylor (eds), *The Theban Necropolis. Past, Present and Future*, pp. 95–121. London: British Museum Press.

Taylor, J. H. 2017. The vulture headdress and other indications of gender on women's coffins in the 1st millennium BC. In A. Amenta and H. Guichard (eds), *Proceedings of the First Vatican Coffin Conference 19–22 June 2013*, vol. 2, pp. 541–50. Vatican: Edizioni Musei Vaticani.

Taylor, J. H. 2018. Evidence for social patterning in Theban coffins of Dynasty 25. In J. H. Taylor and M. Vandenbeusch (eds), *Ancient Egyptian Coffins: Craft Traditions and Functionality*, pp. 349–86. British Museum Publications on Egypt and Sudan 4. Leuven, Paris and Bristol CT: Peeters.

Takabuti's Arrival in Belfast and the First Scientific Studies

Eileen Murphy and Winifred Glover

Takabuti was the first Egyptian mummy to come to Ireland. Her arrival in Belfast in 1834 caused great excitement, and her unwrapping the following year was the equivalent of a modern-day media spectacle.

The mummy and her finely painted anthropomorphic coffin were purchased at a mummy market in Thebes (modern Luxor) by Thomas Greg of Ballymenoch House in Holywood, Co. Down. Many Egyptian tombs were robbed over the years for the benefit of Europeans (Fig. 1). During the fifteenth century it was believed that mummified remains had medicinal properties, but this view had become unfashionable by the eighteenth century, and thereafter mummified remains became prized as the souvenirs of wealthy travellers (Parra 2019). It was fashionable to bring home an Egyptian mummy and unwrap it for the entertainment of one's friends. Greg was a wealthy young man whose father, Cunningham Greg, was the High Sheriff of Antrim in 1828, a post which Thomas held himself in 1840. The reason for his trip to Egypt remains unknown, but it possible he went there as part of the 'Grand Tour' customarily undertaken by wealthy young men at that time as part of their education. This involved an extensive tour through Europe, but some people travelled as far as Egypt. Fortunately, Greg did not keep Takabuti for his personal amusement, but rather presented the mummy to the Belfast Natural History Society for its collections.

1 A mummy vendor resting by his wares in Egypt, 1883.
(photograph by Jean-Gilles Berizzi © Musée du quai Branly – Jacques Chirac, Dist. RMN-Grand Palais / image Musée du quai Branly – Jacques Chirac)

The Belfast Natural History Society was founded in June 1821 by eight young men (Dr James L. Drummond, Professor of Anatomy at the Academical Institution, Francis Archer [aged 18], James Grimshaw, Jr [24], George C. Hyndman [24], James MacAdam [20], William McClure, Jr [19], Robert Patterson, Jr [19] and Robert Simms, Jr), and its purpose was to promote the study of the natural sciences. The original members were later joined by others, including Edmund Getty (aged 22) and the Revd Thomas Dix Hincks, who had been appointed master of the Classical School at the Academical Institution in 1821 and was father of the Revd Dr Edward Hincks, who played a key role in Takabuti's history (see pp. 38–42).

2a Engraving of the Belfast Museum (c. 1831) used in much of its early promotional material.
(PRONI D3263.C.2A)

2b The Belfast Museum today, now more commonly referred to as the Old Museum building.
(photograph courtesy of Ulster Architectural Heritage/Belfast Natural History and Philosophical Society)

In the early years their collections were housed at the Academical Institution and then in rented rooms in the Commercial Buildings in Waring Street. As the collections grew, however, it became clear they needed their own building, and the foundation stone of this was laid by the Marquis of Donegall on 4 May 1830 at a site in College Square North. The building was paid for by public subscription and was officially opened on 1 November 1831 as the Belfast Museum of Natural History (Fig. 2). Funding constraints resulted in the museum not being opened to the public until 1833, but from then it was open on selected days each week. The interests of the members of the Society saw Irish antiquities and more exotic objects added to the collections of natural history specimens. Indeed, so keen was the desire to increase the ethnographic part of the collections that letters of appeal were sent out to 'travellers, merchants, sea captains and Army and Navy officers', who were rewarded for their contributions by being granted free admission to the museum. The body and coffin of Takabuti was a hugely important acquisition for the museum (Nesbitt 1979: 9–11).

The first public mention of the arrival of the mummy was on 12 April 1834, during a talk on Egyptian hieroglyphs at a meeting of the Belfast Natural History Society. The speaker stated that 'the principal object of the writer was to direct the attention of the members to a mummy purchased by a gentleman from this neighbourhood, which was expected to be soon added to the Belfast Museum' (Glover 2006: 404). Also contained in the archives of the Public Record Office of Northern Ireland (PRONI) is a draft letter written on 24 October 1834 thanking Thomas

Greg for his 'highly valuable present of an Egyptian mummy'. Another draft letter to the Revd Dr Edward Hincks indicates that the Society had originally planned to unwrap the mummy on 15 December 1834 but had decided to postpone because they 'found it imperative to have a glass case ready in time for receiving the Mummy after unrolling' (PRONI D3263.B.A.1).

The Unwrapping

Much of what we know about Takabuti's unwrapping depends on the accounts of reporters who witnessed the event, and two main versions were published, one in the *Belfast News-Letter* on 30 January and the other in *The Guardian*, presumably at a similar time, since both were reprinted in various publications over the following days and months. These reprints appeared in publications including *The Dublin Observer, The Newry Examiner, The Newry Telegraph, The Athenaeum Journal of Literature, Science, and Fine Arts, The New Monthly Magazine and Literary Journal* and *Carpere et Colligere: The Museum of Foreign Literature and Science*. Unless stated otherwise, the information below is derived from the *Belfast News-Letter* account.

The unwrapping of Takabuti took place on 27 January 1835 in the upper room of the museum in College Square North commencing at 11 a.m. (Fig. 3). Her 'unrolling' was attended by the eminent men who made up the Belfast Natural History Society and their invited guests, 130 individuals

3 The room in which Takabuti was unwrapped in its current condition in the Old Museum building. The balcony would have enabled those present to get a good view of proceedings.
(photograph courtesy of Eileen Murphy, Queen's University Belfast)

in total. The gravity of the event is captured in the contemporary newspaper accounts, which record that

> the most intense curiosity was depicted on the countenances of all present, when the President had taken the Chair and the mummy enclosed in its case, was laid upon the table. The President then commenced the business of the meeting, by reading from *The Lancet*, a paper descriptive of the unrolling of a Mummy, by the celebrated Dr Granville.

When the lid of the sarcophagus was removed, John Campbell, a teacher of painting who had a studio in Fountain Street, made a colour painting of the wrapped body (Fig. 4). Another bystander, now believed to be Francis Davis, was moved to write a long poem entitled 'On the Mummy in the Belfast Museum', which he had printed on coloured paper with a decorative edge on 9 February 1835 (Fig. 5), and also published in *The Northern Whig* newspaper several days later on 12 February. So captivated was Davis with Takabuti that he published a second poem entitled 'Kabooti; On Musings Ober [Over] a Mummy', amounting to

4 Colour painting of Takabuti in her coffin prior to the unwrapping, made by John Campbell.
(© National Museums NI Collection Ulster Museum)

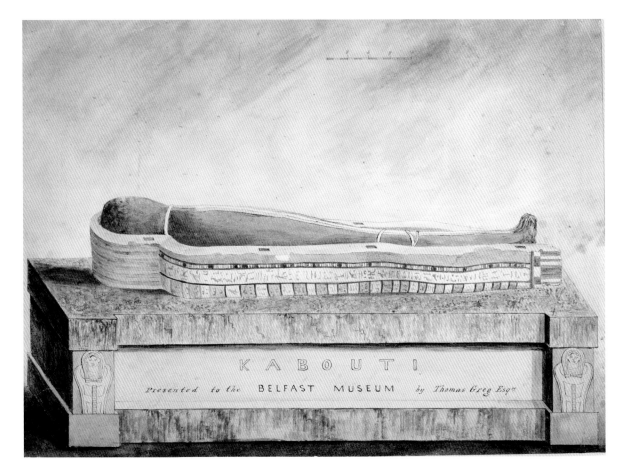

5 Poem about Takabuti written by Francis Davis and published on decorative paper on 9 February 1835.
(PRONI D3263.E.1)

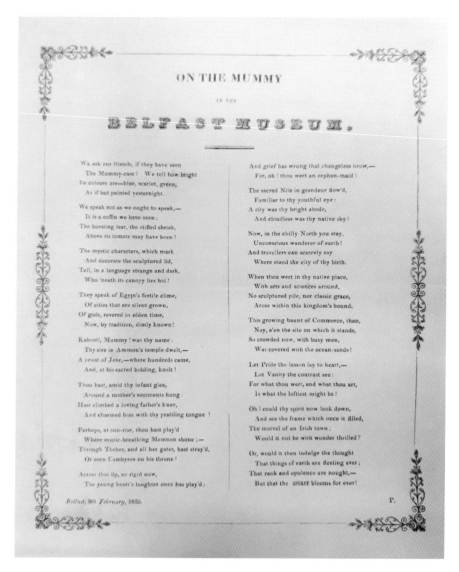

some 11 verses spread over 13 pages, in his book *The Tablet of Shadows: A Phantasy: And Other Poems* published in 1861.

It is reported that four members of the Society – Dr Marshall, Mr Grattan, Mr Getty and the Revd Dr Hincks – were responsible for manipulating the body. First the body was removed from the sarcophagus, and they then proceeded to 'unroll' it. Linen bands, fastened by knots, were untied, and the outer wrapping, which comprised a 'large scarf', buff in colour and 'neatly fringed' with blue beads that were now loose within the case, was removed. This revealed bandages described as 'similar to the bandages used at the present day in surgery, being strips torn from the entire length of the cloth, from 5 to 7 inches wide and about 5½ yards long'. The next layer consisted of wide pieces of cloth folded diagonally across the body and fastened together at the head and feet with 'some glutinous substance'. This was initially removed with alcohol but since the underlying five layers of similar material were heavily encased in the deep brown glutinous substance they were cut away. It was believed the substance would originally have been molten bitumen, and it was recorded that it entirely covered the head, while a compact mass of it filled the space between the shoulders, neck and head (see Chapter 4, pp. 100–101). The limbs were individually bandaged and pledgets of cotton had been placed between the legs and beneath the arms to keep them in their correct position. It was noted that numerous remains of dead insects, but also a living beetle the size of a flea, were discovered during the unwrapping.

The next phase of the process involved an examination of the body. The hair was described as 'being very fine, about 3½ inches long, forming ringlets like those of children, and of a deep auburn shade' (see Chapter 3, pp. 58–61). Interestingly, a lock of her hair was taken at the time of unwrapping, tied with a blue ribbon and kept in a little cardboard box with a glass top (Fig. 6). Today the lock is on display in the Ulster Museum and it still retains the auburn colour described during the unwrapping. It was noted that the eyes had been replaced by 'balls of cotton' (although see Chapter 4, p. 102). The 'lips, cheeks and sides of the head' were described as having suffered from the attacks of insects, the remains of which could still be seen in the holes they had burrowed in the flesh (Fig. 7). *The*

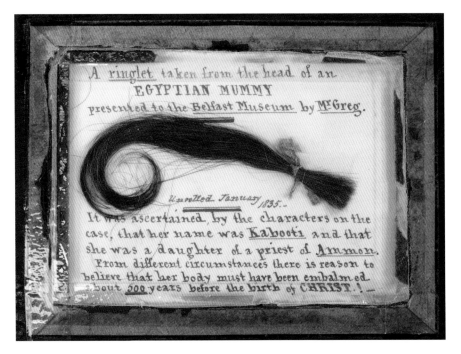

6 Lock of Takabuti's hair taken at the time of the unwrapping in 1835, tied with a blue ribbon and kept in a little cardboard box with a glass lid.
(© National Museums NI Collection Ulster Museum)

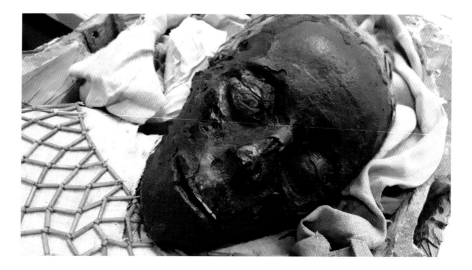
7 Takabuti's head showing
damage caused by insects on
her right cheek.
(photograph courtesy of Eileen
Murphy, Queen's University Belfast)

Guardian account recorded how the lips had originally been tightly compressed and required gentle separation with a knife. The teeth were described as 'white, regular, and very pretty; and, with one single exception, not an unsound one could be seen' (see Chapter 3, pp. 71–72). On the basis of the teeth they determined the age of the individual to have not 'been less than 20, or more than 30'. A phrenological examination of the skull was undertaken by Mr Patterson and Mr Grattan. This would have been particularly fashionable at the time, when it was believed that the shape of the skull could provide information about a person's character and mental facilities. They determined her to have been 'a person of much firmness and caution of character, and of a high degree of intellectual capacity, but little or no taste'. *The Guardian* reporters noted that 'the head and features of the face were rather of a Caucasian than of an African cast'.

Turning their attention to the torso, the sternum and a portion of the ribs were removed and the body was found to have been 'filled with a mixture of powders, probably pounded spices, of a very heavy aromatic odour' (see Chapter 4, pp. 108–10). They observed that the arms lay alongside the body with the hands lying on the upper thighs, and that 'the foot was particularly small, and beautifully shaped'. They measured the length of the body and found it to be 'five feet and one inch long'.

The Guardian account indicates that, following examination of the body, the Revd Dr Hincks gave an explanation of the hieroglyphic figures and inscriptions on the sarcophagus. He was able to say that the coffin contained the remains of a woman named Kabooti (he later revised her name to Takabuti). He estimated that she had lived around 2,000–2,500 years ago and that she had been a daughter of a priest of 'Ammon' (Amun). He determined that her parents were both dead by the time of her death and initially said that she had died unmarried, although this was revised at a later date since the title 'Lady of the House' indicates her married status as the joint owner, with her husband, of a substantial household (see Chapter 1, pp. 17–21). It is interesting to note that in May 1958, Cyril Aldred, the distinguished Egyptologist and author, wrote to the Keeper of Archaeology and Ethnography in the Belfast Museum and Art Gallery, stating that 'If Hincks could read the name of Kabooti (or Takabuti) in 1835 … he must have had a mighty profound knowledge of hieroglyphs for the time, as much as Champollion himself'.

Some of those present at the unwrapping appear to have been given a souvenir of the event. A small envelope marked 'DB' for Day Book p. 136 in the Ulster Museum stores contains a fragment of Takabuti's bandages and a piece of string with some of her faience beads. This is recorded as having been given to 'Francis Davis, "The Belfastman"' at the unwrapping of the mummy, as a souvenir, with a set of two verses by Davis. The verses are not related to Takabuti and the items were donated to the museum by a Miss McLaren who had been given them by Davis's daughter, Mrs McRobie. It is possible that Davis had been given the souvenir bandage and beads as a way of thanking him for the poem he had been inspired to write about Takabuti shortly after her unwrapping.

Early Investigations of Takabuti and her Sarcophagus

Takabuti appears to have undergone an intensive period of study in the month that followed her unwrapping, and an account in the *Belfast News-Letter* on 13 March 1835 reported that a series of papers had been read about the Egyptian mummy at a public session of the Belfast Natural History Society on the evening of 4 March. The event was introduced by Mr Getty who commented on the good state of preservation of the body, contrary to some of the newspaper accounts, before he outlined the order in which the papers were to be presented. A letter from the Revd Dr Hincks was read by Mr R. Simms Jr and provided further details on the hieroglyphs and inscriptions on the sarcophagus, as well as 'much curious information on the superstitions of the Egyptians'. Mr William Patterson remarked upon the colouring of the coffin and concluded that the brightness of the colours should be attributed to the extreme dryness of the climate rather than the skill of the Egyptians. He also exhibited 'a very beautiful and correct' painting he had made of the case as it appeared when first opened, the whereabouts of which is sadly unknown.

Mr William Webb, who worked in the linen trade, had been charged with identifying whether the bandages had been made from linen or cotton. Drawing on previous research, he had examined parts of the cloth under a microscope and compared it with pieces of linen manufactured locally. He concluded irrefutably that all of the material associated with Takabuti had been made using flax fibres and was linen. Mr Patterson discussed the insects discovered during the unwrapping and outlined that they were of two different kinds, and that similar insects had been discovered in other mummies and were those that would have eaten dried flesh and associated materials as opposed to a recently deceased corpse. Professor Stevelly provided a general introduction to the mummification methods used by the ancient Egyptians based on Dr Granville's accounts. He and Mr Grattan had examined a sample of packing material and determined that it comprised 'a mixture of myrrh, benzoin, sloes and some other substances'.

Dr James D. Marshall described the condition of the body, commenting that, despite the insect damage, it was 'in a tolerable state of preservation'. He read a letter from Mr Barnett, a dentist, who was of the opinion that the individual had died at the age of 25–30 years and had teeth that 'were extremely perfect'. The session on the mummy concluded with Mr Patterson reading a paper from Mr Grattan on the phrenology of the mummy, after which he added his own views on the topic.

A later summary of the proceedings published in a volume to commemorate the centenary of the Belfast Natural History and Philosophical Society included a few additional details, noting that Mr George C. Hyndman also spoke with Mr Robert Patterson about the insects, and that Mr Connery focused on the 'workmanship of the case'. It recorded that the dentist involved in the dental examination was William Thompson (Deane 1924: 16). It is a pity that these two short accounts are practically all that remains of these papers today.

A two-page, handwritten 'Analysis of a paper on the phrenological development of the Egyptian mummy read by Mr Grattan' on 4 March 1835 survives in a volume in PRONI (D3263/J/2B). This paper reiterated some of the general characteristics of Takabuti followed by a list of the main cranial features investigated, the deductions from which were summarised as follows: 'character cautious – prudent and determined – virtuous and moral – attached to her friends and fond of children – cheerful – at times satirical – little taste and virtues [?] of mind but much plain common sense'.

The beetles found during the unwrapping of Takabuti attracted a lot of attention, and notes of opposing views on their date were included in the memoirs section of volume 1 of *The Transactions of the Royal Entomological Society of London* published in 1836. It is recorded that Mr Robert Patterson wrote to the Society about the insects recovered during Takabuti's unwrapping. The Revd F. W. Hope, who chaired the Society's meeting during May 1835, was of the view that insects associated with a number of Egyptian mummies, including Takabuti, were alive at the time of mummification. A subsequent letter from Patterson was read at a Society meeting on 3 August 1835 in which he expressed his dissent from Hope's interpretation and gave the opinion that the insects had invaded the body at a much later date, an interpretation that was eventually proven to be correct.

It is interesting that these early nineteenth-century scientific studies were asking many of the same questions as those posed by researchers working on the Takabuti Project almost 200 years later. Who knows what further studies will reveal about her in the future as scientific techniques advance even further.

References

Deane, A. (ed.) 1924. *The Belfast Natural History and Philosophical Society. Centenary Volume, 1821–1921.* Belfast: Belfast Natural History and Philosophical Society.

Glover, W. 2006. Takabuti: Belfast's ancient Egyptian. In M. Meek (ed.), *The Modern Traveller to Our Past: Festschrift in Honour of Ann Hamlin,* pp. 402–08. Belfast: DPK.

Nesbitt, N. 1979. *A Museum in Belfast: A History of the Ulster Museum and its Predecessors.* Belfast: Ulster Museum.

Parra, J. M. 2019. Europe's morbid 'mummy craze' has been an obsession for centuries. *National Geographic*, 12 December, https://www.nationalgeographic.co.uk/history-and-civilisation/2019/12/europes-morbid-mummy-craze-has-been-obsession-centuries (last accessed 21 September 2020).

The Orientalist Revd Dr Edward Hincks (1792–1866)
Gerry Millar

The much-anticipated unwrapping of Takabuti in 1835 by members of the Belfast Natural History Society created huge interest and excitement, but the event was delayed to ensure the presence of one man to decipher the hieroglyphs (see Chapter 1, pp. 32–35). He was not a professor from the British Museum or even a professional Egyptologist. He was a country parson, an amateur Orientalist, the Revd Dr Edward Hincks, Church of Ireland rector of Killyleagh, Co. Down (Fig. 1). Remarkably, some years later he was awarded the Gold Medal by the King of Prussia (a precursor of our Nobel Prize) on the same day as Michael Faraday, one of the world's greatest ever scientists. After his death, Professor Gaston Maspero, the famous French archaeologist and director of the Egyptian Museum in Cairo, commissioned a marble bust of Hincks which was erected in 1906 in the entrance hall of the museum to honour his immense contribution to Egyptology.

1 The Revd Dr Edward Hincks as a young man, artist unknown, oil on canvas.
(reproduced with permission from the Board of Trinity College Dublin, University of Dublin)

This bust is now on display, along with those of other great Egyptologists, in the garden of the museum (Fig. 2). Ironically, his work on Egyptology was not even his greatest accomplishment, which was pioneering the decipherment of the ancient writing and language of Babylon and Assyria known as Akkadian cuneiform.

Hincks was born in Cork in 1792 and grew up in heady and turbulent times, with the 1798 rebellion and the Napoleonic wars. He came from a family of high achievers. His father, the Revd Thomas Dix Hincks, was a professor of Hebrew; one brother became a bishop and another the Prime Minister of Upper Canada and Governor of Barbados. Hincks excelled at Trinity College Dublin, coming first in the entrance exam at the age of 15 and winning many awards. A glittering career in the Church or academia beckoned, but a tendency to be his own worst enemy first showed itself in his youth. Hincks had written a poem praising Napoleon Bonaparte, which was not very diplomatic in wartime, and was viewed all the more negatively since the Duke of Wellington was an Irish aristocrat. In addition, he fell out with two influential men at Trinity – the professor of Hebrew and the Provost, the latter of whom controlled appointments to parishes. Hincks left Trinity and was eventually relegated to a backwater living in Killyleagh, Co. Down, where he remained for 41 years despite many efforts to move to an environment more suitable for undertaking his research (Davidson 1933).

It would be wrong, however, to downgrade the importance of the ministry in his life. It is evident that he was a man of deep faith with a profound sense of duty to his flock. He robustly, but amicably, defended his Church's position in a debate with three Roman Catholic clergy in the Downpatrick Discussion of 1820. Politically, he was a supporter of educational reform and Catholic Emancipation, which again, no doubt, affected his advancement within the Church.

Hincks embarked on his studies of Egypt, Assyria and Babylonia at a time when religious authority was threatened by the Industrial Revolution and new scientific discoveries. Most of the early Egyptian exploratory expeditions were

2a Bust of the Revd Dr Edward Hincks commissioned by Professor Gaston Maspero, the famous French archaeologist who became director of the Egyptian Museum in Tahrir Square, Cairo. This opened in 1902, and in 1906 Hincks's bust was erected in the entrance hall to honour his immense contribution to Egyptology.
(© Belfast Natural History and Philosophical Society, reproduced from Deane 1924: 83)

2b The bust on display today, along with those of other great Egyptologists, in the garden of the Egyptian Museum in Cairo.
(photograph courtesy of Rosalie David, University of Manchester)

funded by religious organisations in order to prove the accuracy of the Bible. In Ireland particularly, where Archbishop Ussher had fixed the date of Creation as midday on 23 October 4004 BC, Hincks's single-minded interest in Egyptian chronology and past astronomical events, which had the potential to challenge the Bible, caused much unease within the Church.

No one doubts that Hincks was a genius, despite his rather absent-minded nature, but he certainly had a complex and multifaceted personality. On the one hand he doted on his daughters and maintained many long-term friends, but he could also be very difficult and scathing to his perceived intellectual inferiors and even to his own brother.

Hincks began work on Old Persian cuneiform to gain new perspective as an Egyptologist, and rapidly made huge progress in decipherment. Ironically, this was from second-hand information trickling into Killyleagh, while his main rival, Colonel Henry Rawlinson, was on site, often dangling from a rope over a cliff edge actually recording the inscriptions. This rivalry escalated over the decipherment of the ancient writings and language of Assyria and Babylon known as Akkadian cuneiform, which followed the discovery of the library, containing tens of thousands of clay cuneiform tablets, of King Assurbanipal at Nineveh in 1842 (Fig. 3).

3 Cuneiform tablet multiples of 270-MAHG 16054 dating to 1800–1700 BC.
(Creative Commons Attribution-ShareAlike 3.0 France (CC BY-SA 3.0 FR), https://commons.wikimedia.org/wiki/File:Cuneiform_tablet-MAHG_15856-IMG_9472-black.jpg)

4 Photograph of the Revd Dr Edward Hincks as an old man. (Creative Commons Attribution only licence (CC BY 4.0), https://commons. wikimedia.org/wiki/File:Edward_ Hincks.jpg)

Hincks and Rawlinson, together with Jules Oppert from France and the photography pioneer William Fox Talbot, soon emerged as the leaders in this new field of Assyriology. However, trying to persuade cautious and sceptical scholars in museums and universities that their decipherment was accurate remained difficult. In 1857 Fox Talbot set up a test that was invigilated by an eminent committee of scholars. An unseen inscription was given independently to Hincks, Rawlinson, Oppert and Fox Talbot and their translations compared. They were found to be very close, especially that of Hincks and Rawlinson, thereby proving the accuracy of their decipherment (Cathcart 2007).

Despite increasing ill health in the latter part of his life, Hincks continued with all aspects of his research, but it is clear from his voluminous correspondence that he worried about the financial security of his family. He also showed increasing disenchantment and suspicion towards the various institutions that did not offer

5 Blue plaque erected
on the wall of Killyleagh
rectory, Co. Down, in 1966,
commemorating the
centenary of the death of the
Revd Dr Edward Hincks.
(photograph courtesy of Gerry Millar,
Queen's University Belfast)

him advancement and support (Cathcart 1994). He died in 1866, and ironically his bitter rival, Colonel Rawlinson, was instrumental in obtaining a pension for his family (Fig. 4).

Edward Hincks exhibited several exceptional gifts that shaped his life. He was a superb linguist, fluent in 13 languages including French, German, Italian, Gaelic, Greek, Hebrew, Latin and Sanskrit. Coupled with this he was a successful codebreaker, winning as a young man an 'unbreakable code' competition prize of £100, a very considerable sum in those days. He was also a published mathematician and highly regarded astronomer. He could therefore see connections and patterns in obscure writings that others could not. He was a 'scholars' scholar' and produced neither any great textbook nor work accessible to the general public to bring him widespread fame and success; nor did he have the people skills to advance his career within the Church or academia. He was hailed as a great man of letters during his lifetime, but there is a marked sense of unfulfilment about him.

His legacy is that he revelled in being a problem solver, and he produced groundbreaking work in Assyriology and Egyptology from his rectory in Killyleagh, despite limited resources, little access to papyri and inscriptions, and never having travelled to the Middle East. His results rivalled and, indeed, surpassed the achievements coming out of the major universities across Europe at the time. A blue plaque was erected on the wall of Killyleagh rectory on the centenary of his death in 1966 in recognition of his great achievements (Fig. 5).

References

Cathcart, K. J. (ed.) 1994. *The Edward Hincks Bicentenary Lectures*. Dublin: Department of Near Eastern Languages.

Cathcart, K. J. (ed.) 2007. *The Correspondence of Edward Hincks 1818–1849, Volume 1*. Dublin: University College Dublin Press.

Davidson, E. F. 1933. *Edward Hincks. A Selection from his Correspondence with a Memoir*. Oxford: Oxford University Press.

Deane, A. (ed.) 1924. *The Belfast Natural History and Philosophical Society. Centenary Volume, 1821–1921*. Belfast: Belfast Natural History and Philosophical Society.

2

Scientific Analysis of Takabuti's Historical Date, Ancestry and Place of Residence

Radiocarbon Dating of Takabuti

Jenefer Metcalfe and Paula Reimer

It is important that, where possible, ancient Egyptian mummies are historically dated and assigned to a particular dynasty or period of Egypt's history. This allows information gathered from scientific studies about the health and lifestyle of a person to be appropriately placed within the correct historical, social and political context. However, this is not always easy to achieve.

Many mummies found in European and American museums today were collected during the eighteenth and nineteenth centuries. During this time, mummies were considered as curios or travel souvenirs by people visiting Egypt as part of the 'Grand Tour' (see Chapter 1, p. 28). These early collectors were not interested in the original context of the mummy, as its value was often only measured in terms of its external appearance or the amulets found within the wrappings. Many mummies were bought in Egypt from local vendors who would collect them to sell to tourists or allow visitors to enter tombs to select a body. The archaeological and historical context of the body was of little or no consequence to the collector. In the absence of such information, other methods must be used to assign a date to a body.

Usually, a range of dating methods are used to verify age. These include assessment of the stylistic date of the coffin (if the mummy has one) based on its shape, method of construction, material, decoration and any hieroglyphic texts. Sometimes radiocarbon dating is used either as an additional method or as a sole dating technique when no other estimate of historical age can be made (Richardin et al. 2013). Artefacts, such as amulets or jewellery, found with the mummy can sometimes also help identify its date. The methods of mummification used may also provide

1 Detail of the bandages at Takabuti's feet. Note the traces of tree rings evident in the adjacent wood of the coffin. (photograph courtesy of Eileen Murphy, Queen's University Belfast)

clues, but certain elements of the process, such as excerebration and evisceration, were used over long periods of time and can only rarely help to provide a precise date (Aufderheide 2003).

Takabuti was brought to Belfast with a coffin, but with no other evidence of date. A previous estimate of the stylistic age of the coffin suggested that she belonged to the 25th Dynasty (c. 755–656 BC) (see p. 24). A series of radiocarbon dates were undertaken on different materials from Takabuti's assemblage – hair from the back of her head, wood from the underside of her coffin, two different pieces of linen wrapping and a sample of the resin extract that formed part of her packing material. These were submitted for analysis at the ^{14}CHRONO Centre for Climate, the Environment and Chronology, Queen's University Belfast, between 2008 and 2019. The purpose of the analyses was 1) to assess the historical age of Takabuti herself (hair sample); 2) to determine whether the coffin and the body belonged together (comparison of hair and coffin samples); and 3) to identify the age of the other funerary materials found with the body (linen wrappings and resin samples) (Fig. 1).

Results

The radiocarbon ages have a broad range (Table 1), clearly demonstrating that Egyptian mummy assemblages can comprise a range of different materials that are not necessarily associated with the date when the individual died or was mummified (Fig. 2). A number of factors can affect the radiocarbon age of archaeological materials, however, and these must be carefully considered.

The hair sample (the only sample taken from the mummy itself) broadly dated to between 794 and 552 BC, falling between the 22nd and 26th Dynasties (931–525 BC) and overlapping with the stylistic age assigned to Takabuti's coffin. At present, it is not possible to be more certain than

Table 1 Radiocarbon dates of a range of materials from Takabuti. Calibration was performed using the OxCal calibration programme (https://c14.arch.ox.ac.uk/oxcal.html).

UBA ref. no.	Sample	Radiocarbon date	Calibrated range (95.4% probability)
18971	Coffin wood	2420 ± 24 BP	733–690 BC (11.4%) 661–649 BC (2.5%) 545–406 BC (81.5%)
10090	Human hair[1]	2531 ± 20 BP	794–746 BC (44.3%) 686–666 BC (13.3%) 644–552 BC (37.8%)
10342	Textile 1	2581 ± 35 BP	818–748 BC (77.9%) 685–666 BC (4.7%) 641–587 BC (9.9%) 581–556 BC (2.9%)
10091	Textile 2[1]	2689 ± 25 BP	896–806 BC (95.4%)
42293	Resin	2746 ± 26 BP	971–960 BC (2.5%) 936–826 BC (92.9%)

[1] These radiocarbon dates were derived from the combination of two replicate dates obtained from the same sample.

this. A liberal coating of embalming materials had to be chemically removed from the hair before it could be analysed (Fig. 3). Following pre-treatment, a carbon to nitrogen (C:N) ratio calculation was carried out to

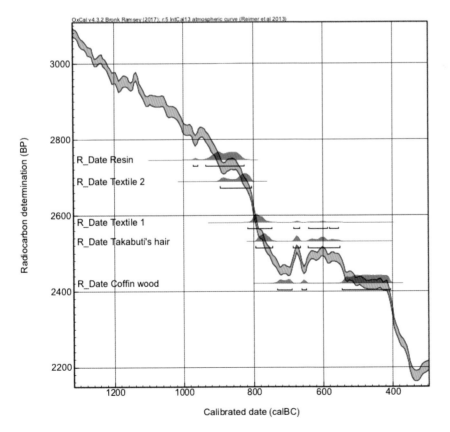

2 A graphical representation of the calibrated ranges for the radiocarbon dates obtained from Takabuti and associated materials.
(prepared by Paula Reimer, Queen's University Belfast)

 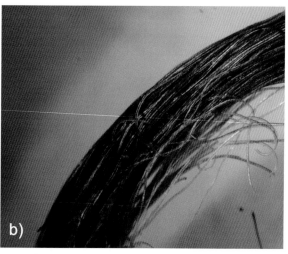

3 Sample of Takabuti's hair used for radiocarbon dating a) before pre-treatment and b) after removal of contaminants. (photographs courtesy of Andrea Klimaschewski, Queen's University Belfast)

check that the keratin was sufficiently well preserved for dating. The ratio was higher than would be expected in modern samples, suggesting that the hair may have undergone some post-mortem degradation or that it had been contaminated. Two radiocarbon dates were produced from the hair which were comparable with each other, but this still does not rule out degradation of the sample.

The wood used to build Takabuti's coffin is again dated to a broad range, but calibration places its most likely date as between the late 26th and 27th Dynasties (664–405 BC). Wood was a valuable commodity in Egypt as the climate did not support the growth of large trees. The wood used for coffins, most commonly cedar wood, was often therefore imported from areas such as modern-day Lebanon. Cedar trees often live for several hundred years, laying down a ring for each year of growth. Each of these tree rings will have its own radiocarbon age, reflective of the year when that growth occurred. As such, the radiocarbon age of a piece of wood used to build a coffin is often older than the body placed within it. These circumstances are not evident with the coffin of Takabuti, however, where the situation is reversed. Assessment of the style by John Taylor from the British Museum dated it to the late 25th Dynasty (see p. 24) and the curators from National Museums Northern Ireland have found no evidence to refute this assessment.

A radiocarbon date younger than the anticipated age of the artefact being dated is usually indicative of contamination by a source of more modern carbon. This can include materials such as modern conservation treatments or varnishes. In the case of Takabuti's coffin, no obvious source of modern contamination was found to be present which could have affected the radiocarbon age of the coffin wood. However, it remains unclear how the coffin has been treated over the years since its arrival in

Belfast in 1834, (see Chapter 1, p. 28) and modern contamination cannot be ruled out with any certainty. In the absence of further radiocarbon or chemical analysis of the coffin, the stylistic criteria used to date it are considered more reliable.

The textiles and resinous material from Takabuti's packing material demonstrate different radiocarbon dates, with age ranges from 896 to 556 BC and from 971 to 826 BC, respectively. Mummies were often wrapped using household or heirloom linens, and embalmers' workshops are likely to have made use of any available old clothing or material. As such, radiocarbon dates for linen samples are often variable (see, for example, Cockitt et al. 2014). They can be broadly comparable with the age of a body or up to a few decades older (as we see with the two textile samples here), or indeed many hundreds of years older in cases where linen from ancient tombs was found and reused.

The resin sample produced the oldest radiocarbon date from Takabuti's funerary assemblage. Materials such as pine or cedar resin have a long growing span and were valuable, imported commodities (see Chapter 4, p. 109). Resin could be transported and stored over a number of years, further adding to its radiocarbon age. The resin would not be expected to have the same age as the body in these circumstances, and an offset of at least 150 years, as seen here, is to be expected.

Summary
The series of radiocarbon dates associated with Takabuti can be seen as a reflection of how the ancient Egyptians imported and used materials. In addition, the data demonstrate some of the complexities associated with interpretation of the results, especially as potential preservation and contamination issues cannot be ruled out with respect to the hair and wood samples. Through the hair sample, Takabuti has been radiocarbon dated to a broad historical period that is comparable with the stylistic age estimation of the mummy and her coffin.

References
Aufderheide, A. C. 2003. *The Scientific Study of Mummies*. Cambridge: Cambridge University Press.

Cockitt, J. A., Martin, S. O. and David, A. R. 2014. A new assessment of the radiocarbon age of Manchester Mummy No. 1770. *Yearbook of Mummy Studies* 2, 95–102.

Richardin, P., Coudert, M., Gandolfo, N. and Vincent, J. 2013. Radiocarbon dating of mummified human remains: application to a series of Coptic mummies from the Louvre Museum. *Radiocarbon* 55, 345–52.

Radiocarbon Dating
Paula Reimer and Jenefer Metcalfe

Isotopes are variants of elements that have the same number of protons and electrons, but a different number of neutrons. This gives isotopes of the same element slightly different atomic masses. Most elements have at least two isotopes and usually one of these is present in a much larger abundance than the other. In most instances, this is the lighter isotope. For example, the 'normal' isotope of carbon is carbon-12 (or ^{12}C), which makes up approximately 99% of all carbon, while carbon-13 (^{13}C) comprises about 1%. The other isotope of carbon, carbon-14 (^{14}C), is radioactive and is only present in tiny amounts.

Radiocarbon (carbon-14) dating can be used to find out approximately when an organism died (Barratt and Reimer 2007; Taylor and Bar-Yosef 2016). This is possible because a radioactive (unstable) isotope of carbon (carbon-14) is created by collisions between nitrogen and fast neutrons produced in the upper atmosphere by cosmic rays. This carbon-14 binds with oxygen to produce carbon dioxide (CO_2) which is taken up by plants through photosynthesis and subsequently eaten by animals and humans (Fig. 1). The carbon-14 survives for a predictable amount of time (known as its half-life) before it reverts back to nitrogen, giving off radiation. While alive the organism continually renews the cells in most tissues but, once it dies, the renewal ceases and the carbon-14 countdown begins. By measuring the amount of carbon-14 remaining, relative to stable carbon, we can calculate a radiocarbon age. By convention the radiocarbon age is calculated relative to AD 1950 and reported as age BP (before present).

Shortly after the carbon-14 dating method was developed, samples of known age were radiocarbon dated as a test. While most of the samples resulted in the expected age, the radiocarbon age of a piece of wood from the Sakkara step pyramid of the Egyptian pharaoh Djoser did not agree with the date given by Egyptologists. Eventually it became clear from dating tree rings of known age that the amount of carbon-14 in the atmosphere had not been constant over time and a correction was needed. A correction or calibration curve was developed, which has been updated many times as more refined radiocarbon measurements of known age material have been made. Calibration of a radiocarbon age was originally done by simply drawing a line from the radiocarbon age axis to intercept the curve and extending that down to the calendar axis. Due to the variations in atmospheric carbon-14 this can result in multiple possible calendar ages. In more recent times, computer programmes have been developed for this purpose.[1] Calibrated ages are reported as cal AD or cal BC where 'cal' stands for calendar or calibrated, to distinguish them from historical ages.

---

1   See http://14chrono.org/radiocarbon-dating/radiocarbon-dating-background/ (last accessed 21 September 2020).

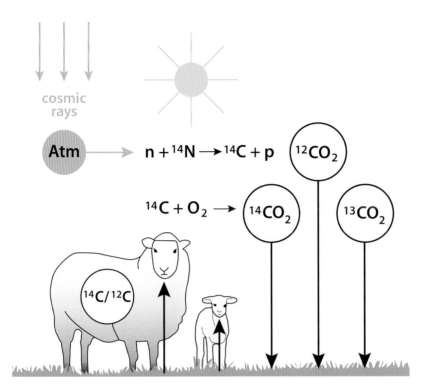

1 The production of carbon-14 in the atmosphere and its incorporation into plants and animals.
(drawn by Libby Mulqueeny, Queen's University Belfast)

cosmic rays

Atm $\longrightarrow$ $n + {}^{14}N \longrightarrow {}^{14}C + p$ ${}^{12}CO_2$

${}^{14}C + O_2 \longrightarrow$ ${}^{14}CO_2$ ${}^{13}CO_2$

${}^{14}C/{}^{12}C$

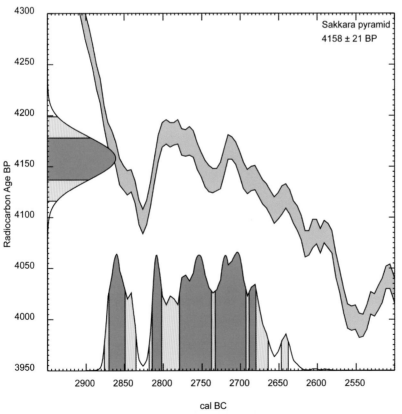

Sakkara pyramid
4158 ± 21 BP

Radiocarbon Age BP

cal BC

2 The radiocarbon and calibrated age range for the Sakkara step pyramid wheat grains at 68% (green) and 95% (yellow) probability. The IntCal13 calibration curve is shown in blue. Calibration was performed with CALIB7.01.
(prepared by Paula Reimer, Queen's University Belfast)

3 Samples for dating undergoing the process of conversion to pure carbon in the 14CHRONO Centre for Climate, the Environment and Chronology at Queen's University Belfast.
(photograph courtesy of Barrie Hartwell, Queen's University Belfast)

4 The accelerator mass spectrometer in the 14CHRONO Centre for Climate, the Environment and Chronology at Queen's University Belfast, undergoing preparation for the analysis of carbon samples.
(photograph courtesy of Svetlana Svyatko, Queen's University Belfast)

A radiocarbon age also has an uncertainty associated with the measurement. This uncertainty or 'error' is given as a ± value to indicate that the age can either be younger or older by the amount stated. For instance, wheat grains from inside the Sakkara step pyramid were recently radiocarbon dated to 4158 ± 21 BP (Dee et al. 2012). In the calibration process, the uncertainty is also included, which results in a calibrated age range of 2880–2630 cal BC at 95% probability for the wheat grains (Fig. 2) which is compatible with the chronological estimation of Egyptologists.

Samples can be contaminated with older or more recent carbon either from the natural environment or from conservation treatments such as wax, glue or varnish previously used in museums. For this reason, the samples have to be carefully cleaned, a process known as pre-treatment. A series of organic solvents followed by distilled water are routinely used for samples that might be contaminated, although it is not always possible to remove some substances completely. After pre-treatment the sample is converted to pure carbon (Fig. 3) and measured by accelerator mass spectrometry (AMS) (Fig. 4)

References

Barratt, P. and Reimer, P. J. 2007. Radiocarbon dating: a practical overview. In E. M. Murphy and N. J. Whitehouse (eds), *Environmental Archaeology in Ireland*, pp. 1–17. Oxford: Oxbow Books.

Dee, M. W., Rowland, J. M., Higham, T. F., Shortland, A. J., Brock, F., Harris, S. A. and Ramsey, C. B. 2012. Synchronising radiocarbon dating and the Egyptian historical chronology by improved sample selection. *Antiquity* 86, 868–83.

Reimer, P. J., Bard, E., Bayliss, A., Beck, J. W., Blackwell, P. G., Ramsey, C. B., Buck, C. E., Cheng, H., Edwards, R. L., Friedrich, M., Grootes, P. M., Guilderson, T. P., Haflidason, H., Hajdas, I., Hatté, C., Heaton, T. J., Hoffmann, D. L., Hogg, A. G., Hughen, K. A., Kaiser, K. F., Kromer, B., Manning, S. W., Niu, M., Reimer, R. W., Richards, D. A., Scott, E. M., Southon, J. R., Staff, R. A., Turney, C. S. M. and Plicht, J. v. d. 2013. IntCal13 and Marine13 radiocarbon age calibration curves 0–50,000 years cal BP. *Radiocarbon* 55, 1869–87.

Stuiver, M., Reimer, P. J. and Reimer, R. W. 2020. CALIB 7.1 online programme, http://calib.org (last accessed 21 September 2020).

Taylor, R. E. and Bar-Yosef, O. 2016. *Radiocarbon Dating: An Archaeological Perspective*. New York: Routledge.

Mitochondrial DNA of Takabuti

Konstantina Drosou

The period from the development of the Mendelian laws of heredity (1865) and the discovery of deoxyribonucleic acid (DNA) by Friedrich Miescher (1869), to Schrödinger's characterisation of the chromosome as an aperiodic crystal and the deciphering of the DNA structure and its information-encoding potential (1952), was an era of radical changes in scientific thought. This resulted in revolutionary insights that would forever change our perception of the universe. These paradigm-shifting events in science signalled the transition from classical genetics to molecular genetics, a new reality. Questions such as how genetics can contribute to the understanding of humans and the environment have triggered the creation of numerous cognate disciplines. The analysis of preserved organisms and ancient remains on a molecular level has created the new scientific field of biomolecular archaeology, thereby opening up an entirely new avenue in evolutionary studies. The fundamental principle upon which biomolecular archaeology is based is that any type of biomolecule, such as nucleic acids, lipids, proteins and even carbohydrates, has the potential, under favourable conditions, to leave traces of organic residues, albeit in a heavily degraded state. Ultimately, this field can provide a unique perspective for the molecular analysis and understanding of several aspects of past life, such as adaptation, plant and animal domestication, migratory routes, palaeopathology, population genetics and ancestry. That premise has led to a remarkable exploration of ancient DNA (aDNA) with regard to the unique information that it can provide and the breadth of archaeological questions that can be potentially answered. Tissue samples were taken from deep within Takabuti's body following established protocols to ensure the samples were not contaminated and that minimal damage was caused to her remains (Fig. 1) (see pp. 83–85).

1 Dr Konstantina Drosou preparing for the aDNA sampling of Takabuti in the Ulster Museum in October 2018.
(photograph courtesy of Keith White, University of Manchester)

The North African Gene Pool

One of the most fascinating topics of research to be addressed in the wake of the aDNA revolution was the evolutionary history and spread of the human species. To this day it is generally accepted on the basis of the Out-of-Africa theory that anatomically modern humans originated in North Africa and spread around the world, most likely through Egypt, about 100,000 years ago (Bons et al. 2019). It is also considered that there were many waves of back-migrations (people who migrated from Africa and then migrated back into Africa) to Africa from Eurasia from 40,000 to 12,000 years ago (Henn et al. 2012). Despite the fact that Egypt has received gene flow from the surrounding regions, Africa has also gone through extensive periods of genetic isolation, resulting in the evolution of the genetically distinct native Berber people. In more recent years, Egypt in particular has had documented interactions with other ancient civilisations in Asia, Europe and the African continent itself. During the first millennium BC Egypt endured a series of foreign dominations by Kushites, Assyrians, Persians, Greeks and Romans. As a result of this, modern-day African populations, including that of Egypt, show a fascinating and intricate gene pool which is difficult to disentangle unless large-scale population genetic studies are undertaken (Fregel et al. 2018).

The scientific debate is still ongoing with regard to the relative contributions of different populations and timelines of gene flow to the current gene pool of North Africans. However, there is a relative consensus, based on genetic data from modern populations, that suggests that the North African gene pool is an amalgamation of four main sources. These comprise an autochthonous Maghrebi population element which probably relates to a back-migration to Africa about 12,000 years ago; a Near Eastern gene flow, probably associated with the Arab conquest (AD 642); a sub-Saharan component derived from trans-Saharan migrations; and a European component related to recent historical population movements. The timing of these migrations is very poorly resolved, however, and shows an extraordinarily complex history of migrations involving at least five ancestral populations into North Africa (Schuenemann et al. 2017, Fregel et al. 2018). Modern studies are not without problems, as results are based on extrapolations and assumptions with regard to ancient datasets. For this reason, ancient DNA is crucial in that it has the potential to provide compelling evidence regarding the population dynamics of ancient Egyptian history and can complement archaeological and historical data.

Human Genome, Genetic Variation and the Use of Mitochondrial Variants in the Identification of Ancestry

Many efforts have been made to shed light on the fascinating history of the African population, and aDNA has been an amazing tool for the identification of genetic variants that could be indicative of past migration routes. Before exploring the aDNA studies undertaken on North African populations to date, and Takabuti's results in particular, it is essential to start with an introduction to key concepts and nomenclature, to help with the understanding of this endeavour.

The human genome is encoded by DNA structured into 23 chromosome pairs that lie within the nucleus of the cells (nuclear DNA). A single chromosome in each pair is inherited from each parent. However, a small part of the genome exists outside the nucleus of the cell, within the mitochondria, and is usually referred to as the mitochondrial genome, to distinguish it from the nuclear genome. Mitochondrial DNA (mtDNA) is an extremely useful tool in aDNA studies, because it exists in multiple copies per cell, in contrast to the nuclear DNA which exists in only two copies per cell (apart from the Y chromosome which has only one copy). This means that it can be more easily recovered from degraded sources such as archaeological bones, teeth, mummified soft tissue remains and more. Most importantly, mtDNA has an exclusive maternal mode of inheritance which means that, by analysing mitochondrial genomes through time and space, we can observe its evolution in real time.

As a result of the Human Genome Project (HGP) more than 20,500 human genes have been sequenced and more than 98% of the entire human genome is now known. This breakthrough involved more than 2,000 researchers around the world, and took 11 years to complete. Having a complete sequence of the human mitochondrial genome as a reference sequence (known as the revised Cambridge

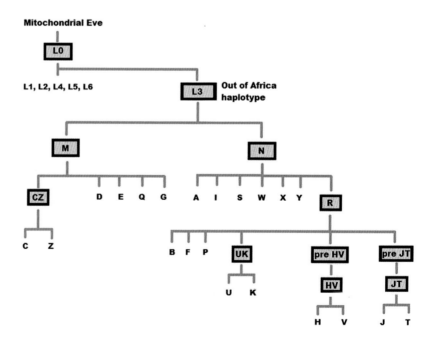

2 Simplified diagram showing the evolutionary relationships of the different haplogroups.
(Creative Commons Attribution-ShareAlike 3.0 Unported (CC BY-SA 3.0), https://commons.wikimedia.org/wiki/File:MtDNA_tree.jpg)

Reference Sequence – rCRS), to which all human sequences can be compared, has resulted in aDNA studies becoming very popular. Consequently, efforts have been made to reconstruct the genetic pathway of human evolution by tracing the most recent common ancestor (MRCA), known as 'mitochondrial Eve'. This was made possible through the comparative study of genetic variation (Fig. 2). But what is genetic variation?

Genetic variation is essentially a set of differences in the DNA sequence between individuals and populations. Different individuals have different profiles of variation; however, certain genetic variants are prevalent in different human populations. The presence or absence of genetic variations and the way they are arranged in specific positions within the genome can be considered as a molecular 'black box'. As such, they have the potential to provide information on several aspects of past human lives, such as population migrations, domestication, familial relationships and ancestry. Humans are about 99.6% genetically identical to each other, which means that only 0.4% of the genetic information can differentiate us from each other. However, because the genome is vast, this 0.4% means that every human has several million variants in comparison to the reference genome sequence. Variation found in that 0.4% provides genetic markers which can be used to differentiate between ancestral populations. In the field of aDNA, the best genetic marker for ancestry identification is the single nucleotide variation (SNV), which represents a change in a single position (nucleotide) within the genome (Fig. 3).

Most SNVs have no effect on health and development; for example, initial studies into healthy human populations identified that the average person's DNA sequence will contain several hundred variants predicted to knock out the function of known genes, as well as a few tens of variants previously associated with genetic diseases. Because variation is therefore normal and natural, the Human Genome Variation Society specified that the term 'variant' should not be confused with the term 'mutation', which is often used to denote a variant associated with a deleterious effect. Similarly, the term 'variant' should not be confused with the term 'polymorphism', which is generally used to denote a variant with a benign effect.

Single nucleotide variants are advantageous in aDNA studies because of the degraded nature of DNA. A complete set of variants in an individual's mitochondrial DNA is called the haplotype. In terms of aDNA population studies, a haplotype is defined by the combination of various common

3 A single nucleotide variant (SNV) in a single base-pair location in the genome. (amended from copyrighted work available under Creative Commons Attribution 4.0 International (CC BY 4.0), https://en.wikipedia.org/wiki/Single-nucleotide_polymorphism#/media/File:Dna-SNP.svg)

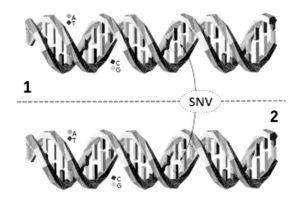

SNVs. These haplotypes fall into approximately 90 broad geographical categories, known as haplogroups. Each individual possesses a certain number of these polymorphisms (haplotype) from which their category (haplogroup) is defined. These haplogroups have nested sub-haplogroups depending on the different observed haplotypes. For example, if two individuals possess a specific mitochondrial haplotype that is grouped into the same haplogroup, that means they share a common maternal ancestor.

Takabuti's Mitochondrial Footprint

As it currently stands, haplogroup U6 is considered an 'autochthonous' North African lineage and, together with the M and L haplogroups, they constitute the majority of the genetic footprints of the first and second millennia BC, expanded by J2a, R0, T1, T2 and HV during the first millennium BC. These are found in various frequencies within the African population. Examination of Takabuti's genome showed a set of polymorphisms which together belong to a rare mitochondrial haplogroup – H4a1 (Drosou et al. 2020) (Fig. 4). The H macro-haplogroup is

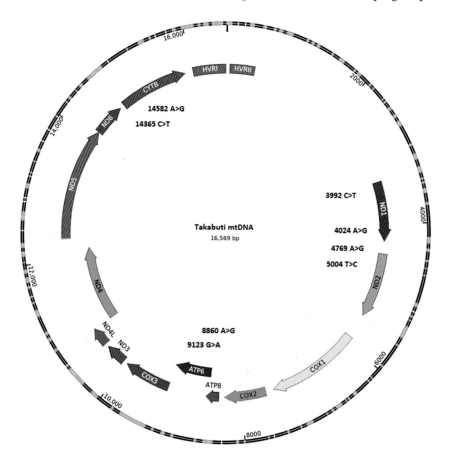

4 Takabuti's mitochondrial genome with key SNVs. Arrows indicate gene positions. The outer circle represents DNA coverage; black parts indicate that DNA is preserved; red parts indicate missing data.
(© Konstantina Drosou. Image created via SnapGene)

the most common mtDNA haplogroup in Europe today and is also found in parts of present-day Africa and Asia. H4 in particular, together with H7 and H13, is found in about 42% of the modern Egyptian population. The H4a1 variant possessed by Takabuti appears in low frequencies in modern populations in southern Iberia, Lebanon and the Canary Islands. In an ancient context, H4a1 has been reported in samples from the Canary Islands (fourteenth–sixth century BC); three samples from Bell Beaker and Únětice contexts (2500–1575 BC) at Quedlinburg and Eulau, both in Saxony-Anhalt, Germany; and in a small number from Early Bronze Age Bulgaria. Previous examination of 97 samples from ancient Egypt shows a complicated society with a rich mixture of genetic backgrounds. Takabuti's genetic results were able to enrich this database in that, until now, the H4a1 haplogroup has not been found in any modern or ancient Egyptian samples. This shows that single case studies can also add to our current knowledge of haplogroup distribution and can act as a starting point for further large-scale population genetic studies.

References

Bons, P. D., Bauer, C. C., Bocherens, H., de Riese, T., Drucker, D. G., Francken, M., Menendez, L., Uhl, A., van Milligen, B. P. and Wiβing, C. 2019. Out of Africa by spontaneous migration waves. *PloS One* 14, e0201998. doi:10.1371/ journal.pone.0201998.

Drosou, K., Collin, T. C., Freeman, P. J., Loynes, R. and Freemont, T. 2020. The first reported case of the rare mitochondrial haplotype H4a1 in ancient Egypt. *Nature: Scientific Reports*, 10 (17037).

Fregel, R., Mendez, F. L., Bokdot, Y., Martin-Socas, D., Camalich-Massieu, M. D., Santana, J., Morales, M., Avila-Arcos, M. C., Underhill, P. A., Sharpiro, B., Wojcik, G., Rasmussen, M., Soares, A. E. R., Kapp, J., Sockell, A., Rodriguez-Santos, F. J., Mikdad, A., Trujillo-Mederos, A. and Bustamante, C. D. 2018. Ancient genomes from North Africa evidence prehistoric migrations to the Maghreb from both the Levant and Europe. *Proceedings of the National Academy of Sciences of the United States of America* 115, 6774–79.

Henn, B. M., Botigue, L. R., Gravel, S., Aang, W., Brisbin, A., Byrnes, J. K., Fadhlaoui-Zid, K., Zalloua, P. A., Moreno-Estrada, A., Bertranpetit, J., Bustamante, C. D. and Comas, D. 2012. Genomic ancestry of North Africans supports back-to-Africa migrations. *PloS Genetics* 8, e1002397. doi:10.1371/journal.pgen.1002397.

Schuenemann, V. J., Peltzer, A., Welte, B., van Pelt, W. P., Molak, M., Wang, C.-C., Furtwangler, A., Urban, C., Reiter, E., Nieselt, T., Francken, M., Harvati, K., Haak, W., Schiffels, S. and Krause, J. 2017. Ancient Egyptian mummy genomes suggest an increase of sub-Saharan African ancestry in post-Roman periods. *Nature Communications* 8, article number 15694.

Takabuti's Hair
Natalie McCreesh and Andrew Gize

The mummified remains of Takabuti were intact from the day she was embalmed until 1835 when she was 'unrolled'. Therefore her body and hair were protected from the elements by layers of bandages and resin for c. 2,500 years. The hair is described in the *Belfast News-Letter* account of 30 January 1835 as being 'in excellent preservation, being very fine, about 3½ inches long, forming ringlets like those of children, and of a deep auburn shade, with not the slightest appearance of wool'. A lock of her hair was taken at the time of unwrapping, tied with a ribbon and kept in a little box, a custom of the Victorian era. Today the lock is on display in the Ulster Museum and it still retains the auburn colour described; however, the hair on Takabuti's head now has a yellow-orange colour, probably due to the long exposure to the air since the time of her unwrapping (see Chapter 1, p. 33) (Fig. 1).

Also noted during the unwrapping of the mummy was the large number of beetles that had penetrated the wrappings, attacking the body, especially the head, and more so on the sides. When the beetles were first able to access the body is unknown, but it was reported that they had perforated the skin. The mummy was fumigated with Phosphine gas in 1987 for conservation. Having such records allows an idea of the condition of the hair to be anticipated in advance of further research. We were aware there might have been damage caused by insects in addition to degradation through oxidation due to exposure after the unwrapping. The colour of ancient hair is often affected by degradation and mummification procedures, and cannot be presumed to represent its original colour. Takabuti is an excellent example of how hair can degrade, as evidenced

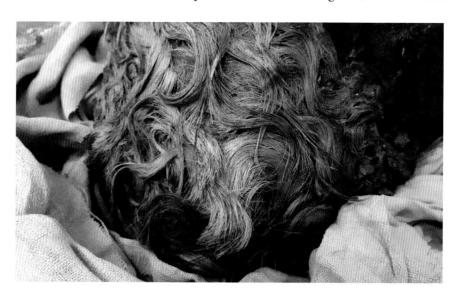

1 Takabuti's hair today with yellow-orange discoloration, probably due to the long exposure to the air since the time of her unwrapping in 1835.
(photograph courtesy of Eileen Murphy, Queen's University Belfast)

in the marked differences in the condition of the hair samples taken in 1835 and 2008. Hair is an extremely stable structure and is resistant to decomposition and enzymatic digestion, resulting in it often being the least degraded part of mummified human and animal remains. Taking a sample of hair is much less intrusive or destructive than more frequently examined samples, such as skin and bone, yet a wealth of pathological and social information can be gained from it (McCreesh et al. 2011a).

Microscopy and chemical analysis previously undertaken on hair samples from other mummies has provided a wealth of information on mummification procedures, life in ancient Egypt and the pathology of hair (McCreesh et al. 2011a; 2011b). Examination of the hair cuticle can be used to assess the presence of disease and state of nutrition. Mechanical factors affecting the hair, such as the use of hair dye and styling, can also be explored. In ancient Egypt the hair was typically treated post-mortem along with the body as part of the funerary rituals. This included the use of oils and unguents for anointing, in addition to the application of preservatives as part of the embalming process. Social status was often reflected in the quality of the burial and the level of embalming. The analysis of hair is carried out with the aim of gaining a greater understanding of an individual's life and identity (McCreesh et al. 2011a).

Materials and Methods

At the University of Manchester in May 2008 small samples of Takabuti's hair were taken – fragments of approximately 3 cm by 1 cm were taken from the mid-point of the back of the head using tweezers (see Chapter 3, p. 88). A further two substantial curls of hair, one with scalp possibly attached, and approximately 6 cm in length were then taken in the Ulster

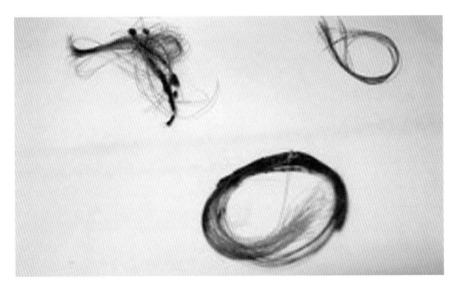

2 The main hair sample included in the study. Analysis was focused on the lock in the foreground. The sample was removed with tweezers and thus the ends are left uncut and in their original condition, as specified via sampling requirements. Residue is evident on the mid-section of the curled lock. This was analysed via gas chromatography mass spectrometry (GC-MS) and has been identified as the fixing agent. Debris, such as dust, has also become attached to the hair.
(photograph courtesy of Natalie McCreesh, University of Manchester)

Museum in July 2008. In addition to the hair tied with a ribbon and placed in the box in 1835, the Ulster Museum had other hair samples from this time stored away and a longer sample of this hair, approximately 7.5 cm in length, was also included in the study (Fig. 2).

Light microscopy and environmental scanning electron microscopy (ESEM) were employed to visually examine the samples (Fig. 3). Following thermal desorption of approximately 1 mg of hair, gas chromatography-mass spectrometry (GC-MS) was used to separate and identify substances in the complex mixtures that had been applied to it. The use of a microscale analytical technique ensured minimal damage to the samples (see Gize 2008).

Results and Discussion
Takabuti's head hair appears, macroscopically, pale blond with a dry, straw-like texture. As mentioned above, a lock of hair was taken from the mummy when it was originally unwrapped in 1835, and stored in a container. This hair retains a darker, auburn colour and has a much smoother appearance. It is possible to compare the condition of this relatively protected hair with the samples taken directly from Takabuti's

head. Microscopically, the exposed hair is not well preserved; it is coated in fungal matter and dust, and has become weak, breaking easily. Major signs of physical degradation are cracks and nodes evident in the hair (Fig. 4) that may be the result of general oxidation or insect attack. The cuticle is visible in areas not damaged or covered in debris and is intact and lies flat, with smooth scales characteristic of healthy hair. Evidence of a smooth coating on some parts of the hair (Figs. 5 and 6) has the appearance of an oil or fat. The lock of hair taken at the time of unwrapping and preserved separately is in a much better condition. The hair is not as dry and has no evidence of degradation, such as the weathering of the shaft, visible in the sample taken from her head in 2008. An amount of debris covers the surface but not to the extent of the other sample. The cuticle is visually clearer and represents that of healthy hair (Fig. 7). Pigment retained at the root of the hair indicated the original hair colour to be dark. Cross sections of the hair indicated it to be Caucasian in shape.

The hair displayed mainly blunt cut tips, slightly smoothed in some strands, with broken tips on others (Fig. 8), which indicated it had been cut relatively close to the time of death. This interpretation is derived from the occurrence of the slightly rounded tips, since the hair would have had very straight tips (if cut with scissors) if it had been cut post-mortem. This interpretation, however, is based on comparison with modern examples. The presence of many broken hairs may indicate that the implements used were simply blunter than their modern counterparts. If the hair tips had been very elongated, into a point, this would indicate it had not been cut for some months prior to death since, once hair has been cut, the tips start to round and eventually elongate.

4 Fracture/damage to the hair as seen using light microscopy. (image courtesy of Natalie McCreesh, University of Manchester)

5 Hair coating as seen using light microscope. (image courtesy of Natalie McCreesh, University of Manchester)

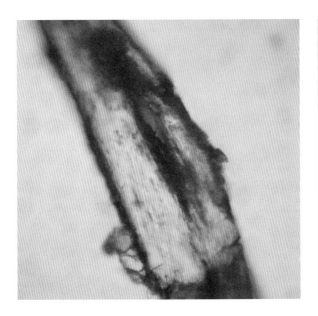

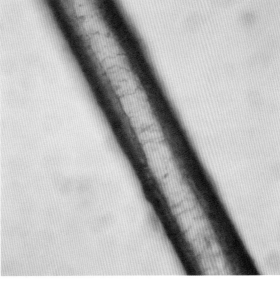

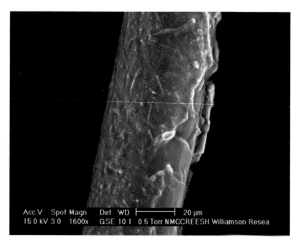

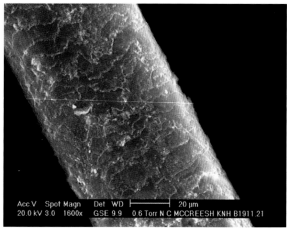

Acc.V Spot Magn   Det WD ├──────┤ 20 µm
15.0 kV 3.0 1600x   GSE 10.1 0.5 Torr NMCCREESH Williamson Resea

Acc.V Spot Magn   Det WD ├──────┤ 20 µm
20.0 kV 3.0 1600x   GSE 9.9   0.6 Torr N.C MCCREESH KNH B1911.21

6 Hair coating as seen using environmental scanning electron microscopy. The cuticle is visible where the hair is not coated.
(image courtesy of Natalie McCreesh, University of Manchester)

7 Environmental scanning electron microscopy revealed that the hair cuticle was well preserved, indicating that Takabuti had healthy hair in good condition.
(image courtesy of Natalie McCreesh, University of Manchester)

8 The tips of the hair are straight/horizontal in a squared shape, which is indicative of recently cut hair as seen using transmitted white light microscopy. a) width of view 2µm, b) width of view 100µm.
(images courtesy of Natalie McCreesh, University of Manchester)

The hair was shorter at the front (approximately 7 cm long) than the back and was worn in a high chignon style. It had been set into neat artificial curls, and it is presumed some form of agent must have been applied to hold it in place. It is possible that the curls were artificially created using a heated instrument, but the curl would not have held that position for very long without some form of fixative. The residue on the hair, which formed a smooth coating over it microscopically, may have been applied as a hair fixative, to hold the style in place. A similar hair-styling technique has been previously reported on mummies from the Dakhleh Oasis (McCreesh et al. 2011b).

GC-MS analysis indicated the nature of all of the volatile compounds present in the hair sample (Fig. 9), but with no associated dating evidence. Recent contaminants are likely to comprise phthalate esters derived from plastics (peaks 3, 7 and 8) and silicone grease. Optical microscopy suggested the presence of a colourless coating on the hairs. The absence of regular peaks of straight chain hydrocarbons is not compatible with beeswax as a major component of the coating and suggests that a natural fat had been applied to coat the hair. Recent fats are characterised

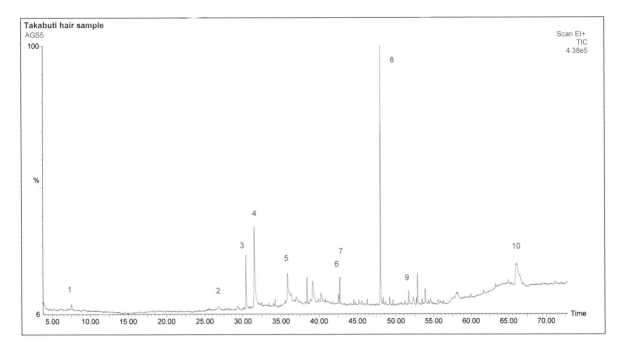

Scan EI+
TIC
4.38e5

8

4

3

5

7

6

10

9

1

2

Time

5.00   10.00   15.00   20.00   25.00   30.00   35.00   40.00   45.00   50.00   55.00   60.00   65.00   70.00

9 Total ion current chromatogram (TIC) of Takabuti's hair. The peaks indicate: 1 – camphor, 2 – tetradecanoic acid, 3 – phthalate ester, 4 – hexadecanoic acid, 5 – octadecanoic acid, 6 – dehydroabietic acid, methyl ester, 7 – phthalate ester, 8 – phthalate ester, 9 – cholesterol and 10 – silicone grease. (© Andrew Gize)

by labile unsaturated carboxylic acids, but these compounds are absent from the sample, indicating that the saturated carboxylic acids could represent the residue of the original anointing material.

Noteworthy is the presence of two compounds, camphor (peak 1) and dehydroabietic acid methyl ester (peak 6). Camphor was used by ancient Egyptians as an antimicrobial agent during embalming. A direct source of the methyl ester of dehydroabietic acid is not known, but pyrolysis from abietic acid is a possible source (Haken 2000). Abietic acid occurs in the resin of conifers.

It was reported in 1835 that Takabuti's mummy had been infested by insects, although it was questionable as to whether these were modern or ancient (see Chapter 1, pp. 33–34). A possible louse or nit egg was found attached to one hair strand, but without further investigation of additional samples it is not possible to say definitively that she had suffered from nits. When examined under a microscope it appeared to resemble a louse egg due to the characteristic oval shape cemented to the hair shaft, although this cannot be considered conclusive due to the small sample size. As lice can only survive on a living scalp, any lice or their eggs positively identified would have been from ancient times. Takabuti, like many of her ancient Egyptian contemporaries, may well have suffered with head lice. Remedies from ancient Egypt for the treatment of lice are similar to traditional methods used today. The hair is covered with an oil to suffocate the lice which, along with the eggs, are then removed by a fine-toothed comb.

Conclusion

In summary, it is fair to say that Takabuti's body was tended to with great care at or around the time of her death. Her hair was neatly cut and was carefully curled and styled into a high chignon. The hair of many mummified individuals is often heavily coated with embalming unguents, but Takabuti's carefully tended hair was largely left free, perhaps so that it was not disturbed. The agent used to hold her curls in place appears on the roots to mid-hair shaft, which is where most of the debris has attached, suggesting that it may have had a sticky or soft composition, like a fat-based substance. It is intriguing to wonder if this is how she would have had her hair styled during life, since the aim of mummification was to make the body resemble as closely as possible the deceased's appearance when alive. Many mummies have been found with closely shaven heads and it is presumed that they would have worn wigs. It is possible that Takabuti also wore a traditional wig, perhaps for more formal occasions, and that the curled and styled hair we see today was an appearance she adopted for everyday wear. Having her hair arranged in this manner for burial is a likely indication that this is how she looked in daily life.

References

Gize, A. P. 2008. An introduction to analytical methods. In R. David (ed.), *Egyptian Mummies and Modern Science*, pp. 133–61. Cambridge: Cambridge University Press.

Haken, J. K. 2000. Synthetic polymers – gas chromatography. In I. D. Wilson, M. Cooke and C. F. Poole (eds), *Encyclopedia of Separation Science*, pp. 4334–43. New York: Academic Press.

McCreesh, N. C., Gize, A. P., Denton, J. and David, A. R. 2011a. Hair analysis: a tool for identifying pathological and social information. In H. Gill-Frerking, W. Rosendahl and A. Zink (eds), *Yearbook of Mummy Studies vol. 1*, pp. 95–98. Munich: Verlag Dr Friedrich Pfeil.

McCreesh, N. C., Gize, A. P. and David, A. R. 2011b. Ancient Egyptian 'hair gel': new insight into ancient Egyptian mummification procedures through chemical analysis. *Journal of Archaeological Science* 38, 3432–34.

3

Takabuti's Age, Health and Diet

Imaging Takabuti: Radiology and Osteology
Eileen Murphy, Robert Loynes and Judith Adams†

The body of Takabuti had not undergone any thorough scientific study since it was unwrapped in 1835. As such, a core component of the modern research was to undertake non-invasive imaging to see if more could be learned about its physical characteristics and the mummification processes (see Chapter 4, pp. 100–106). In 1987 a series of X-rays were taken of Takabuti by Dr David Heylings, using a portable machine from the Department of Anatomy at Queen's University Belfast. Although the portable X-ray machine had limitations, it still managed to provide images sufficiently detailed to provide information on mummification techniques (a resin 'collar'), post-mortem damage to the body (a phalanx or finger bone in the chest, damage to the sternum), and salient characteristics of the skeleton (e.g. lumbarisation – the first sacral segment not being fused with the second and appearing as part of the lumbar vertebrae). Subsequent analysis was undertaken in May 2008 as part of the research for the BBC Northern Ireland documentary *Show Me the Mummy: The Face of Takabuti*, which involved the body making the journey across the sea to Manchester (see Chapter 1, p. 5). It was transported to the Manchester Royal Infirmary where, under the direction of the late Professor Judith Adams, it underwent a programme of radiography (Fig. 1) and multi-detector computer tomography (Fig. 2). A series of radiographs was taken which included views of the skull, chest, abdomen, upper legs, lower legs and feet similar to those taken in 1987. The multi-detector computed tomography (CT) involved taking some 2,756 scans of 0.6 mm thick slices through the body. Recent analysis of the Dicom file using more modern software has revealed further information about Takabuti's mummification and cause of death (see Chapter 4, pp. 91–95; pp. 100–106).

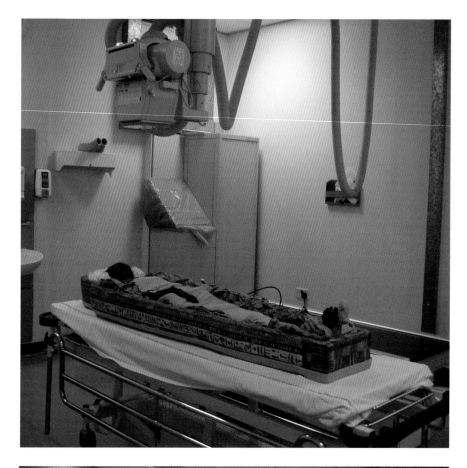

1 Takabuti undergoing radiography in Manchester Royal Infirmary in May 2008. (photograph courtesy of Eileen Murphy, Queen's University Belfast)

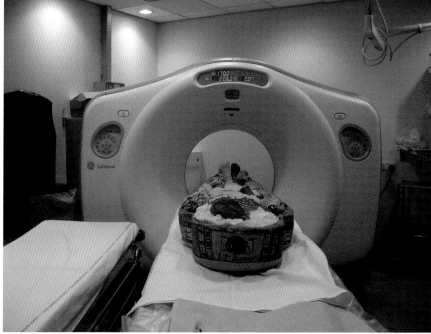

2 Takabuti undergoing multi-detector computer tomography in Manchester Royal Infirmary in May 2008. (photograph courtesy of Eileen Murphy, Queen's University Belfast)

Biological Profile

Using information derived from the radiographs and CT scans it was possible to use standard osteological methods to determine the sex, age at death and stature of the skeleton (see Schwartz 1995; Raven and Taconis 2005). The hieroglyphs on the sarcophagus indicated that it had been made for a woman named Takabuti (see pp. 24–27), but it was necessary to ensure the body was actually that of a female, as coffin reuse was a common feature in several eras of ancient Egypt. Soft tissue indicators of the sex of the mummy are no longer present. The newspaper accounts of her unwrapping describe how during the latter stages of removal of the bandages, 'One leg, the arms, the upper part of the breast, and the head were now completely exposed to view'. When they mention 'breast', however, it is possible they are referring more generally to the chest area and assuming the body was female due to the appearance of the coffin and the content of the hieroglyphs.

Adult male and female skeletons have a number of differences, with those in the pelvic region most pronounced due to the adaptation of the female pelvis for pregnancy and childbearing. The male skull and joints also tend to be more robust, but these observations are less reliable for sex determination. Radiography of the abdominal area revealed a gynaecoid pelvis, confirming the body was that of an adult female. This type of pelvis has a round pelvic inlet and a shallow pelvic cavity, with a wide sub-pubic angle. Takabuti's sub-pubic angle was in the region of 100° and her greater sciatic notches were also wide, with angles of 84°, both characteristically female features. The cranium also displayed typically female characteristics. The glabellar profile was smooth and frontal bossing was noted, while the nuchal area of the back of the cranium was also smooth, with no evidence of ridging, and the skull had an overall shape that was gracile and rounded (Fig. 3).

When Takabuti was originally unwrapped and studied in 1835 it was concluded from the appearance of her teeth that she was not less than 20 or more than 30 years old when she died. The imaging analysis has confirmed this, since all 32 of her teeth were fully erupted, indicating adulthood. The presence of minimal wear on the occlusal (biting) surfaces of the molars might extend her age to the mid-30s. Examination of the state of fusion of the sternal ends of the clavicles and fusion between the centra of the first and second sacral vertebrae were suggestive of an age-at-death in the late 20s or early 30s. No signs of osteoarthritis were evident in her bones, further suggesting that she died when she was a young adult.

During the 1835 unwrapping the body was measured as 5 feet and 1 inch long. Using mathematical osteological methods, based on the measurement of the femur and tibia, her estimated living stature

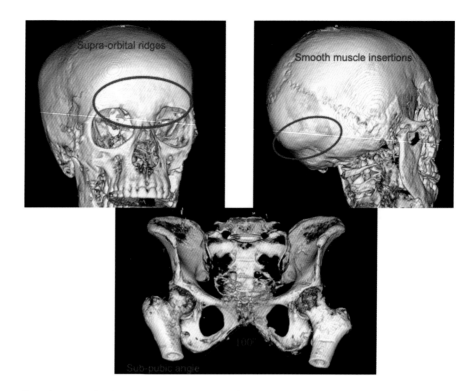

has been calculated as approximately 158–59 cm. Her stature can also be determined by measuring the body on the CT scan images, and this approach indicated that she had a height of 159 cm (5 feet 2 inches).

Health

There were no obvious signs of disease in Takabuti's skeleton, though only certain conditions leave markers in the skeleton. Scans of the legs revealed a degree of asymmetry in which the soft tissues of the right leg were slightly less robust than those of the left leg. While this might have been caused by disease, it could also have been due to the natural asymmetry evident in all living creatures. The lumbarisation of the first sacral vertebra identified in the 1987 X-ray was confirmed in the 2008 CT scan. This is a congenital deformity of no great health significance that affects about 2% of the modern population. It is interesting that she also displayed a dental congenital anomaly (see Chapter 3, p. 71).

Post-Mortem Damage to the Body

We know from the newspaper accounts of 1835 that the unwrapping of Takabuti involved an intrusion that damaged her sternum and the adjacent ribs (see Chapter 1, p. 34). The imaging revealed both this and further evidence of damage that had occurred since her mummification. A major gap was visible between the fifth lumbar vertebra and the first

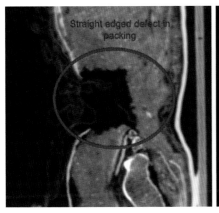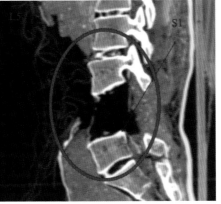

4 Damage to the abdominal area, possibly caused during the 1835 unwrapping.
(© R. D. Loynes and the University of Manchester)

sacral segment that extended right across her abdomen, including the packing material within, indicating that the damage had occurred after mummification. It is impossible to know when this happened, but it seems probable that it occurred during the 1835 'unrolling'. The very straight profile of the damaged edges of the packing material indicates a deliberate removal of the material (Fig. 4). Takabuti's left hand also displayed damage which involved dislocation of the fingers from the hand. None of this damage is described in the 1835 account.

Conclusion

The osteological analysis of the body revealed that Takabuti was a petite woman with a stature of around 158–59 cm who died in her late 20s or early 30s. No definite signs of disease were evident in her remains beyond a minor congenital anomaly. Her mummy appears to have been damaged at some stage after the mummification process, most likely during the 1835 unwrapping.

References

Raven, M. J. and Taconis, W. K. 2005. *Egyptian Mummies: Radiological Atlas of the Collections in the National Museum of Antiquities in Leiden*. Papers on Archaeology of the Leiden Museum of Antiquities 1. Turnhout: Brepols.

Schwartz, J. H. 1995. *Skeleton Keys: An Introduction to Human Skeletal Morphology, Development and Analysis*. Oxford: Oxford University Press.

Takabuti's Teeth

Roger Forshaw

An odontological examination was undertaken of Takabuti's teeth, as such studies can furnish a wealth of information about the deceased person. They can provide direct evidence of the individual's diet; they can provide data that contributes to our understanding of health and disease in antiquity; and teeth have the potential to provide information about social and cultural behaviour.

There are a number of difficulties when attempting to examine the teeth of a mummy, the main problem being that of adequate access. A visual inspection is usually possible when analysing skeletal remains but, when examining mummified and often wrapped bodies, it is necessary to utilise imaging techniques to investigate internal structures such as the teeth (see Chapter 3, pp. 83–85).

Takabuti was mummified and sealed inside her coffin some 2,500 years ago, and then unwrapped at the time of the 1835 investigations, which resulted in the teeth becoming partially visible (see Chapter 1, p. 34). The inflexible and leathery nature of mummified tissue prevents the mouth from being opened to allow a full view of the teeth (Fig. 1). With Takabuti it was just possible to insert a dental mirror into the partially open space between the teeth and examine their occlusal, palatal and lingual surfaces. This inspection together with information derived from radiographic and CT scanning techniques permitted a certain amount to be learned about her dentition.

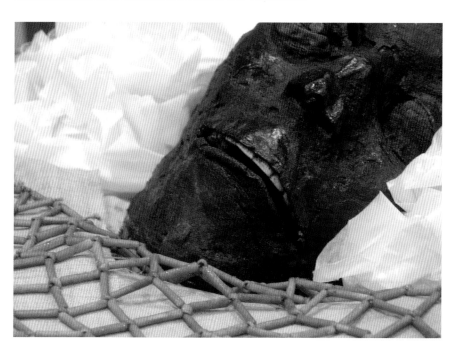

1. The appearance of Takabuti's teeth in her mummified remains.
(photograph courtesy of Eileen Murphy, Queen's University Belfast)

Characteristics of the Teeth

The results of the examination indicate that the aesthetic appearance of Takabuti's teeth was good, with no spacing and a regular symmetrical alignment. All of the teeth were present and none were malpositioned. The four third molars (wisdom teeth) were erupted with the roots fully formed, suggesting a minimum age of 18–25 years at the time of death (Hillson 1996: 136–37).

One interesting feature was the presence of an additional tooth – an extra incisor – in the midline of the mandible (Fig. 2). As the tooth resembles the other mandibular incisors, it can be regarded as a supplemental tooth rather than a supernumerary tooth which is abnormal in form. Supernumerary teeth, commonly present in the midline of the maxilla, have a modern incidence of around 2%, but mandibular supplemental teeth are quite rare, with current rates of 0.01%–0.02% suggested. Their cause is uncertain but they may be the result of a partition of the tooth bud when the teeth are developing. Genetics may also have a role in the occurrence of this anomaly. Takabuti's appearance would not have been compromised by the abnormality and her occlusion appears to have been normal. As such, the additional tooth would have been of little or no consequence to her.

Only one example of caries (tooth decay) was evident in the mouth of Takabuti and this comprised a buccal cavity in the left maxillary third molar (Figs. 3 and 4). Caries occurs as a result of the breakdown of refined carbohydrates in the diet, particularly sucrose and fructose, by bacteria

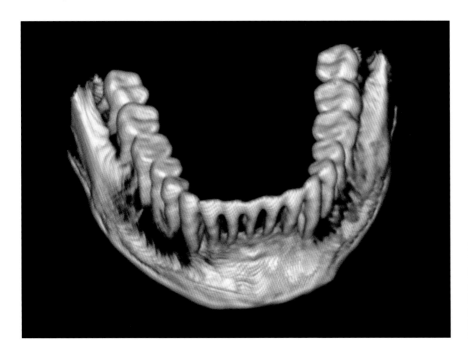

2 3D reconstruction of Takabuti's mandible from the CT Dicom file, showing the supplemental incisor (five incisors can be seen rather than the customary four).
(© R. D. Loynes and the University of Manchester)

3 Orthopantomogram from the CT Dicom file of Takabuti's maxillary teeth showing a buccal carious cavity in the left third molar.
(© R. D. Loynes and the University of Manchester)

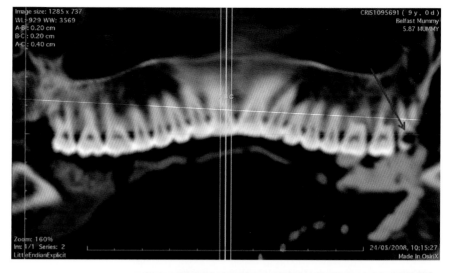

4 CT scan and 3D reconstruction of the maxilla from the CT Dicom file showing a buccal carious cavity in the left third molar.
(© R. D. Loynes and the University of Manchester)

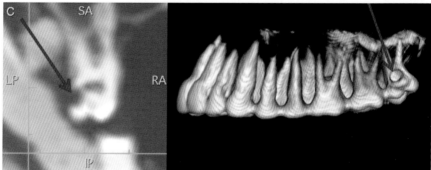

found in the plaque deposited on teeth. Caries was present in ancient Egypt but, throughout most of the Dynastic period, the prevalence was fairly low due to a lack of consumption of these refined carbohydrates (Forshaw 2009: 423).

There was little indication of periodontal (gum) disease in Takabuti and no deposits of calculus were evident on the teeth. The primary cause of periodontal disease is bacterial irritation brought about by the accumulation of deposits of plaque and calculus (calcified plaque) at the gum margin, usually due to poor oral hygiene. The deposits cause inflammation and destruction of the gums, followed by loss of bony support for the teeth and possible subsequent tooth loss.

The writings of the fifth-century BC historian Herodotus indicate that hygiene was important in ancient Egypt, and evidence for the elite suggests that much of the population washed every day, with cosmetics and perfumes an important part of life for both sexes (see Chapter 1, pp. 20–21). Numerous cosmetic and toilet articles have been discovered in ancient Egypt, but nothing resembling a toothbrush has ever been found. Some form of wooden toothpick may well have been used, since other civilisations in antiquity are known to have used various implements, such as chew sticks, tree twigs, birds' feathers, animal bones and porcupine quills for cleaning the teeth (Forshaw 2009: 423). Perhaps something resembling a miswak was utilised, this being a twig of the *Salvadora persica* tree whose ends have been frayed. The miswak is reputed to have been used by the ancient Babylonians; it is known to have been used for oral care by Muslims since the birth of Islam and, indeed, is still in use today (Al Sadhan and Alma 1999). It is possible that Takabuti used such an oral hygiene aid since her teeth were in such good condition.

The radiographic and visual examination of Takabuti's teeth indicated minimal tooth wear (Fig. 5). Many ancient Egyptian teeth were worn down quite rapidly from an early age due to the contamination of food, predominantly bread, their staple diet, with large numbers of inorganic particles (see Chapter 1, pp. 21–22). These fragments rapidly abraded the enamel and subsequently the underlying dentine of the tooth. The particles would have originated from various sources, but primarily comprised sand blown in from the desert. Contamination would also have occurred due to fracturing of the flint-toothed sickle harvesting tools in use in ancient Egypt, as well as the ingress of particles from the soil where the grain grew. In addition, grinding the grain with soft sandstone implements and baking the bread on the outside of stone ovens would have further contributed to this process (Miller 2008: 24).

The lack of tooth wear in Takabuti could relate to the particular diet she consumed. As the daughter of a priest, she may have been given various

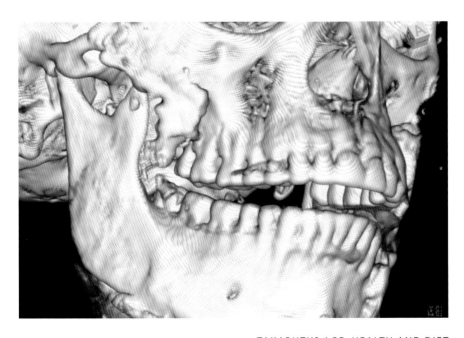

5 Minimal wear evident on Takabuti's teeth.
(© R. D. Loynes and the University of Manchester)

foodstuffs by her father. Food offerings would have been presented to the god associated with the temple each day. After a period of time, when it was considered that the deity had partaken of the essence of the food, it would have been removed from the divine presence and distributed to the priesthood for their personal consumption (see Chapter 1, p. 21). The varied foodstuffs would almost certainly have been of high quality and consisted of items such as meat, fruit and vegetables. This high-protein diet, with vegetable and fruit content, would not have caused the same degree of tooth wear as a diet predominantly consisting of contaminated bread.

Conclusion

Takabuti, who probably only lived into her late 20s or early 30s, a short period by today's expectations, was fortunate in having teeth that seem largely to have been trouble-free. This would not have been the case for many of her fellow ancient Egyptians, who suffered from worn, sensitive and abscessed teeth, and who would have experienced toothache as part of their everyday lives.

References

Al Sadhan, R. and Alma, K. 1999. Miswak (chewing stick): a cultural and scientific heritage. *Saudi Dental Journal* 11, 80–88.

Forshaw, R. 2009. Dental health and disease in ancient Egypt. *British Dental Journal* 206, 421–24.

Hillson, S. 1996. *Dental Anthropology*. Cambridge: Cambridge University Press.

Miller, J. 2008. *An Appraisal of the Skulls and Dentition of Ancient Egyptians, Highlighting the Pathology and Speculating on the Influence of Diet and Environment*. BAR International Series 1794. Oxford: Archaeopress.

Takabuti's Health: Techniques and Findings

Anthony Freemont and Davide Chasserini

Part of the 2018 programme of research involved the application of 'discovery' proteomics to a sample of skeletal muscle obtained from Takabuti. This is a new technique in the field of ancient mummy studies. This section will provide a review of techniques from molecular patho-biology that can be applied to ancient human and animal remains before focusing on the study of Takabuti.

Concepts of Health

'Health' and 'lack of health' are facets of modern lives that are generally regarded as hugely important. Scarcely a day goes by without the media detailing aspects of disease and how to lead healthy lifestyles. To our modern society there are obvious examples of a lack of health (e.g. cancer, infection, dementia) when defining health and disease, but can the same be said for ancient societies and for Takabuti in particular?

Since 1948 the World Health Organisation has defined health as 'a state of complete physical, mental and social well-being and not merely the absence of disease or infirmity'.[1] At first sight, this definition has the advantage of referring to the individual and therefore not requiring a comparator. However, how often has any one of us considered ourselves to be in 'a state of *complete* physical, mental *and* social well-being', and how can we tell if someone from an ancient society met all these criteria? Disease is even more complex to define. The *Oxford English Dictionary* has many definitions, but the most pertinent to us are: 'A condition of the body, or some part or organ of the body, in which its functions are disturbed or deranged; a departure from the state of health'. It follows from these definitions that to understand disease one has to recognise normal function and health.

In 1761 Morgagni, the Italian anatomical pathologist, published his momentous work *De Sedibus et Causis Morborum per Anatomem Indagatis – Of the Seats and Causes of Diseases Investigated Through Anatomy*. This was the first real recognition of disease originating within and affecting organs. Since then we have been searching to better understand, classify and manage disease using 'evidence-based medicine'. This approach makes diagnostic, prognostic and therapeutic decisions using evidence from well-designed and well-conducted research. For much of the documented history of disease and its management, the evidence base for diagnosis and therapeutics is missing from the record. Arguably, the

---

1 https://www.who.int/about/who-we-are/frequently-asked-questions (last accessed 21 September 2020).

Edwin Smith Papyrus indicates that, at least in the area of trauma, there was a rational approach to patient management in ancient Egypt. In the 'golden age of Islamic medicine', during the ninth to eleventh centuries, evidence-based medicine was widely advocated. However, at no time in history have technological advances directed understanding of health and disease as they do currently.

From Morgagni's day to the present, there has been an evolution of ideas about the primary abnormalities underlying disease. While continuing to attempt to understand disease at the level of the organ, during the nineteenth and twentieth centuries there was a move towards understanding disease by studying cellular interactions and abnormalities and using techniques including histology (the examination of slivers of tissue under the microscope). Today we are avidly investigating the molecular basis of disease.

This is the background against which scientific mummy studies now advances. Mummies are important in bioarchaeology, because soft tissues, not just bones, are preserved. Egyptian mummies are particularly important because of their number, state of preservation and the timeframe they span, essentially from the Predynastic Period to the fall of the Roman Empire, c. 3200 BC–AD fourth century. There are also other important aspects to such studies, key among which is a real concern that in the search for knowledge and understanding we pay due respect to the bodies we are examining. The study of samples of Takabuti's tissues bore all these considerations in mind.

Investigative Techniques

Autopsy, although providing a huge amount of information about an individual, is highly invasive, and histology requires a similarly intrusive approach. Techniques such as imaging using CT scans are completely physically non-invasive and provide large amounts of key information (of which Takabuti is a good example). Sampling for molecular studies requires only very small amounts of tissue (a few milligrammes of dry tissue) and can be obtained using needle biopsy or sometimes endoscopy, in which a thin telescope is passed into a space within the mummy and a biopsy taken using fine forceps passed down the microscope (~10 mg of tissue) (Fig. 1). Both procedures require making a small incision (~0.2–1 cm long) in the skin and wrappings (see pp. 83–85).

Examination of the organs, particularly bones, but also 'soft tissues' underpinned the understanding of health and disease in ancient Egyptian mummies from the early nineteenth century, and continues today. For instance, histological examination of minute tissue samples taken from Asru, a mummy curated in the Manchester Museum, uncovered

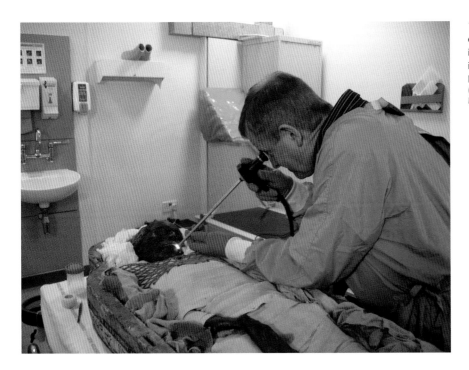

1 Ken Wildsmith using an endoscope to examine the interior of Takabuti's mouth in the Manchester Royal Infirmary in 2008.
(photograph courtesy of Eileen Murphy, Queen's University Belfast)

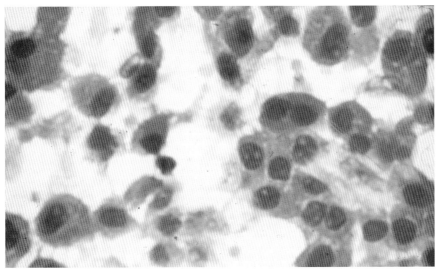

2 Cancer cells, probably from multiple myeloma, in tissue artificially mummified using natron x1000. The mummified tissue was left for five years in a dry, warm atmosphere before processing. There is a reasonable level of cellular preservation.
(© Anthony Freemont, University of Manchester)

three different worm infestations – strongyloidiasis in the intestinal wall (Tapp 1979), schistosomiasis in the bladder (Rutherford 2008) and a hydatid cyst (the larval form of a tapeworm) in the lung (David and Tapp 1984). At the time this information could not have been obtained in any other way. Michael Zimmerman (1977), using skills acquired over many years of research in human pathology, has histologically identified tissue changes indicative of infection, cancer (Fig. 2) and inflammation in ancient Egyptian and other human mummified remains; again, these could not have been identified in any other way at the time. There are many other examples of valuable data that have contributed to understanding the normal burden of disease in ancient Egypt. Histological material removed from Takabuti in 2008 by Ken Wildsmith confirmed that the structural components of the tissue were normal, but that cellular preservation was lacking, even in the skin. No evidence of decomposition caused by anaerobic bacteria (which come from the bowel) was evident in her remains and this may reflect evisceration shortly after death and the subsequent success of the mummification process. However, in the future, as the quality of imaging improves and skills are gained from working on living people, techniques such as CT targeted biopsy could be used, for instance to sample similar diseased tissues to those observed in Asru, without the need to unwrap the mummy or perform an autopsy.

So how can techniques from molecular pathobiology help us understand health and disease and the people and cultures of ancient Egypt (or indeed the rest of the ancient world)? For this it is necessary to know what is possible. The molecules that can be looked for are:

Nucleic acids: Of the two main groups, RNA and DNA, RNA is unlikely to be preserved, but DNA is more durable. DNA, although degraded, does survive in archaeological material (see Chapter 2, pp. 52–57). It is of two types, mitochondrial and genomic. Because the ovum provides the cytoplasm of the single-celled embryo, the maternal line provides all mitochondrial DNA. Genomic DNA can be defined by its chromosomal origin. DNA is an inherited blueprint and it can reveal a lot about ancestry (e.g. finding the H4a1 haplogroup in Takabuti), but cannot indicate whether a person has a disease. The exception to this occurs in well-defined genetic disorders, such as trisomies, in which cells have three copies of a gene instead of the usual two, for example trisomy 21 which defines Down syndrome. In the modern world, genomic analysis can indicate whether an individual is at risk of developing a disease; for example, possession of the harmful mutation of the BRAC1 gene is known to increase the likelihood of developing breast cancer from 12% to about 70%, and there is no reason to believe that this cannot be extrapolated to ancient people and societies.

Proteins: These are molecules made using DNA blueprints. There are many different types of protein molecules, all of which 'do' something and are key to how cells, tissues, organs and the entire body behave. So proteins make up the skeletons of cells; they are the main component of bones, tendons, muscles, cartilage, skin; they recognise molecules that are foreign to the organism (e.g. infective agents, someone else's kidney);

3 Schistosomes stained by immunohistochemistry x400. (courtesy of P. Rutherford, University of Manchester)

they are used by cells to tell others when and how to work; they carry other molecules around the body (e.g. haemoglobin carries oxygen); in fact they are involved in just about everything that is, and that happens, within the body. Examining them provides different but complementary data to DNA. It is possible to look for proteins in histological sections using a technique called immunohistochemistry (e.g. identifying schistosomes by making proteins only found in the organism clearly visible) (Fig. 3).

Lipids (or fats): These are present in the human body and in the foods we eat. They are essential to the way cells work; their membranes are mostly comprised of lipids. Changes in the lipid composition of cells can provide information about the manner in which they may be dysfunctional. To date, the study of lipids in ancient settings has largely focused on the identification of food remains in the interior of pottery vessels.

Sugars: Sugars (e.g. saccharides and carbohydrates) are a complex group of molecules that have structural, lubricating and signalling roles. They are water soluble and are often quickly lost during decomposition, but can be preserved in dehydrated remains, such as desiccated mummified tissues. Very little literature exists on the examination of saccharides in mummified tissue.

Proteomics

Part of the 2018 programme of research involved the application of 'discovery' proteomics to a sample of skeletal muscle obtained from Takabuti, and this produced some exciting results. We will start with some background to introduce this technique. Proteins are large, complexly folded molecules consisting of chains of building blocks called peptides. Peptide order is specific for individual proteins and small changes can increase or decrease protein function. In addition, some peptides have short side chains protruding from them (Fig. 4). There are different types of side chains, which also affect protein function. Changes in peptides and/or side chains can occur after the protein has been built and even after the individual has died. One change, called deamidation, can confirm the authenticity of the protein as 'ancient'. This is important knowledge, as samples can be contaminated with 'modern' proteins from people handling samples, or from the environment in which the research occurs. We undertake 'discovery' proteomics, which makes the very most of the sample, and allows information on several thousand proteins to be gained from modern tissue.

The proteins in the skeletal muscle sample obtained from Takabuti were degraded to a certain extent. This was not unexpected, as full mummification takes time, during which natural degradation is bound

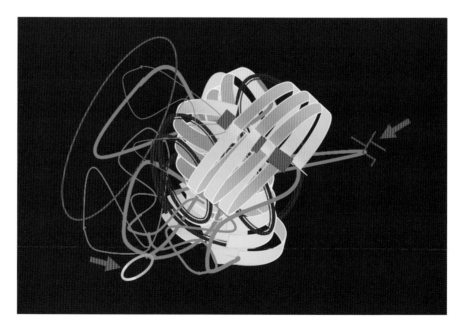

4 A diagrammatic example of the structure of a protein. There is a dense, highly convoluted core of complexly wrapped peptide chains. Protruding from the surface are more loosely coiled peptide chains (within the magenta oval) that represent the protein's 'binding region' by which it attaches to other proteins to initiate a tissue or cell reaction. The magenta arrows point to small side chains. These changeable components affect the coiling of the protein and the structure of the binding region.
(© Anthony Freemont, University of Manchester)

to occur. The results indicated that this was the sort of degradation that occurs in the body and was not decomposition caused by bacteria and other organisms. Using the most modern technology available to study peptides and computer-based informatics that allows reconstruction of complete proteins, it was possible to reconstruct 324 key ancient proteins in the sample from Takabuti. This may not seem many but, from the protein perspective, skeletal muscle is a relatively simple structure. Among the most important proteins identified were structural molecules, including different forms of actin and myosin, the main contractile elements of muscle. Enzymes essential for making muscles work were also identified, particularly those that move calcium in and out of cells, essential since calcium regulates muscle contraction. All of these appeared to match those found in 'normal' muscle today, making it unlikely that Takabuti had suffered from a muscle disease. Muscles are highly vascular organs and part of the sample also included blood proteins. None of the inflammatory proteins reported in modern people who are dying of infection or inflammatory diseases were identified in the sample from Takabuti.

In addition to the ancient proteins recognised by their levels of deamidation, proteins from fungi and bacteria were also identified, and these represented the normal types of organisms associated with mummy wrappings. Other forms of variation in side chain and peptide structure were identified, but none were abnormal or unexpected (Hendry et al. 2018).

Conclusion

We are fortunate to be living at a time when modern technology allows huge amounts of information to be gained from targeted sampling of tiny amounts of tissue. Autopsy and histology provide science with the maximum opportunity to understand disease and those aspects of a culture represented within tissues and molecules. Material retrieved in this way from the past is a unique resource, and the ethical and practical issues raised through the use of these techniques should be at the forefront of our minds when considering future approaches to gaining an understanding of ancient Egyptian people and cultures from human tissues.

The 'discovery' proteomics approach used in the current study, employing techniques used every day in live patients, can be used to generate valuable data in many areas of pathobiology, as the type and structure of proteins change in every disease. In live people they can tell us whether an individual has an infection or cancer, whether they are malnourished, even whether they have diseases of the nervous system.

There is no reason to suppose that this does not also apply to ancient individuals. Takabuti's muscle studies show exactly the wealth of information that can be obtained from studying the proteome in mummified tissue.

The information gained using proteomics is complementary to other techniques, such as the examination of ancient DNA, and adds an extra dimension to understanding physiology and disease in mummies. For instance ancient DNA technologies can tell us if an organism such as a bacterium is present in the tissue, but only proteomics can tell us if the organism was causing an infection or just sitting there. A good example is the number and diversity of bacteria we have in our bowel (the microbiome) which are there but not causing an infection, while another example might be the identification of whether someone was infected by or 'just carrying' typhoid.

Takabuti has taught us much about what is possible; adding her data to that already existing from other individuals enriches our scientific knowledge and understanding of ancient Egypt.

References

David, R. and Tapp, E. (eds) 1984. *Evidence Embalmed: Modern Medicine and the Mummies of Ancient Egypt.* Manchester: Manchester University Press.

Hendry, J., Welker, F., Demarchi, B., Speller, C., Warinner, C. and Collins, M. J. 2018. A guide to ancient protein studies. *Nature Ecology & Evolution* 2, 791–99.

Rutherford, P. 2008. The use of immunocytochemistry to diagnose disease in mummies. In R. David (ed.), *Egyptian Mummies and Modern Science*, pp. 99–115. Cambridge: Cambridge University Press.

Tapp, E. 1979. Disease in the Manchester mummies. In R. David (ed.), *The Manchester Museum Mummy Project: Multidisciplinary Research on Ancient Egyptian Mummified Remains*, pp. 95–102. Manchester: Manchester University Press.

Zimmerman, M. R. 1977. An experimental study of mummification pertinent to the antiquity of cancer. *Cancer* 40, 1358–62.

Retrieval of Tissue Samples
Robert Loynes and Mark Regan

Although CT scans and X-rays provide a non-invasive method of investigating mummies and mummification, there are circumstances when obtaining samples of tissue from the mummy is necessary. Such investigations include ancient DNA analysis, proteomics, stable isotope analysis, histology (including electron microscopy), radiocarbon dating, as well as the chemical analysis of hair, packing material, resin and unguents. All of these techniques were applied to Takabuti.

After initial identification of suitable targets for sampling using the CT scan images it was necessary to devise a strategy to obtain samples in the most effective and least damaging way. Fortunately, the above-mentioned analyses can be performed on very small quantities of tissue/material, with the necessary samples requiring a weight of a few milligrammes or, at most, a few tens of milligrammes.

In the case of Takabuti, samples could be obtained using either direct access or a needle biopsy. Direct samples of hair and bandage were taken during 2008 for radiocarbon dating, stable isotope analysis and the chemical and histological analysis of the hair. In the 2018 study additional direct samples of hair and resin from the neck area were acquired for stable isotope and chemical analysis. A needle biopsy approach was necessary so that samples could be obtained from deep within the body, with vertebral bodies or bulky muscles (in the upper thigh) being especially useful sources of material. This particular type of target tissue was chosen to minimise the possibility of contamination, essential when sampling for aDNA analysis (see Chapter 2, pp. 52–57).

On 8 October 2018 Robert Loynes performed the deep tissue biopsies with the aid of Mark Regan. Three targets were selected – the vertebral

1 The X-ray C-arm image intensifier used during the needle biopsy sampling of Takabuti undertaken in the Ulster Museum in 2018.
(© National Museums NI, Collection Ulster Museum)

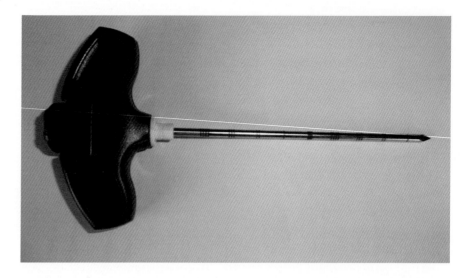

2 A bone biopsy needle with an external diameter of 3 mm.
(photograph courtesy of R. D. Loynes)

bodies of the lumbar spine, the posterior muscles of the right thigh and the packing material located within the trunk (in the para-spinal gutters). In order to accurately reach these targets with minimal damage to the body, it was necessary to use an X-ray C-arm image intensifier, a piece of equipment commonly used in an operating theatre (Fig. 1). Prior to sampling, the targets were confirmed in two planes (A/P – from front to back and lateral – from the side). A bone biopsy needle was used to retrieve the tissue samples. This had an external diameter of 3 mm and collected samples with a diameter of 2.4 mm (Figs. 2 and 3).

3 Mark Regan pointing out the bone biopsy needle within Takabuti's spine on the X-ray machine during the sampling undertaken in the Ulster Museum in 2018.
(photograph courtesy of Eileen Murphy, Queen's University Belfast)

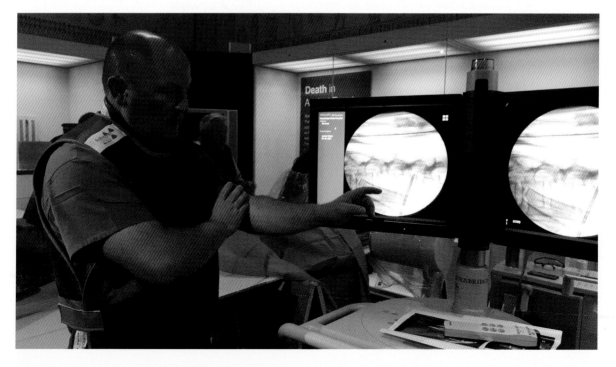

It was possible to introduce the needle into the body through the inner linen bandages in an area where the bandage was normally folded over. The outer bandages were held back by a retracting hook during the sampling process and the point of entry was then hidden when the bandages were restored to their original positions (Fig. 4). As the needle has a cutting point it was possible to drill through the bone while, at the same time, collecting a core sample of tissue/material. Several samples were collected for each investigation so that the need for repeat collection was minimised.

The first samples to be collected by needle biopsy were for aDNA analysis, and the need to minimise any chance of contamination with modern human DNA was crucial. The entire team in the vicinity of the mummy wore forensic coverall protective suits while these samples were being collected. After collection, the specimens were placed in sterile containers so that they could be safely stored for their journey to the different laboratories for analysis. As a matter of good practice, the points of sample collection were recorded on X-ray images for future reference.

4 Dr Robert Loynes using a retracting hook to hold back the outer bandages before inserting the bone biopsy needle to take samples from within Takabuti's spine in the Ulster Museum in 2018. (photograph courtesy of Keith White, University of Manchester)

Stable Isotopes and Takabuti's Diet

Jenefer Metcalfe and Paula Reimer

Stable isotope analysis can be used to study the diet of ancient populations, as well as providing information about their health status and the climate and environment in which they lived (Katzenberg 2000). The isotopic study of bone samples can provide information about the long-term protein source of an individual's diet, but hair provides a much more recent indicator. Any dietary change in the months immediately prior to death would be identified using this approach. Although the analysis cannot identify the precise cause of any variability, the reasons for dietary change can include factors such as illness, seasonal availability of food resources or movement between regions.

Studies of samples of archaeological human bone using this method have been around since the 1970s, but a lot less research has been carried out on other materials, such as hair, especially from mummified bodies. The mummy of Takabuti offered a rare opportunity to conduct an isotopic study of the carbon and nitrogen isotopes preserved in her hair. Although a significant number of ancient Egyptian mummies have been previously unwrapped, relatively few have been found with remaining hair.

Carbon and Nitrogen Isotope Analysis

Carbon-14 (^{14}C) is used by archaeologists to date organic materials, but the analysis of carbon-13 (^{13}C) is also extremely useful. This is because the elements required to create new proteins, and ultimately build and renew body tissues, come from the diet. The marginally different rates of reactions between isotopes mean that at each stage in the food chain their proportions change very slightly, but in a predictable and measurable manner. The amount of carbon-13 in a cow, for example, is slightly different to that in the grass that it eats, while the quantity in the person who eats meat derived from the cow is slightly different to that of the cow.

Plants form the basis of every person's diet, both directly through their consumption or, indirectly, through eating animals that eat the plants. Although a huge range of plants are eaten by humans and animals, there are only a small number of ways that plants turn carbon dioxide from the air into sugars and other molecules. This allows us to distinguish between temperate plants, such as wheat and barley (C3 plants), and plants that thrive in more arid conditions, such as sorghum and maize (C4 plants). By analysing the stable carbon isotope ratios of a person's tissues we can tell what sort of crops they grew for themselves and their animals (Fig. 1). An entirely C3-based diet in an omnivorous human would involve the consumption of C3 plants and animal protein sources (e.g. meat, milk, blood, marrow etc.) from herbivores that also consumed a C3-based diet.

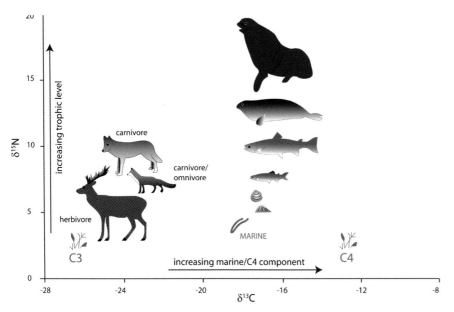

1. Representation of stable isotope values (δ^{13}C and δ^{15}N) for typical dietary resources. (adapted from Schulting 1998, with permission from the author)

The analysis of the stable isotopes of nitrogen is also very useful for those studying ancient diet. Unlike carbon isotopes, these do not provide information on where the food chain starts, but instead indicate how high up the food chain an animal or human was situated. The proportion of the heavier isotope of nitrogen, nitrogen-15 (^{15}N), increases predictably with each step up the food chain (known as trophic level). This allows a determination to be made of roughly how much animal protein (including dairy products), as opposed to plant matter, was consumed (see Fig. 1). The identification of fish and other aquatic food sources is sometimes possible using nitrogen isotopes, in particular. This is potentially very valuable for studies of the ancient Egyptian population, as the archaeological record attests to the consumption of freshwater fish from the Nile.

Sampling and Analysis

Two sets of hair samples were taken from Takabuti and submitted for isotopic analysis – a bulk hair sample taken from the back of the head and a 6 cm strand taken from the midline forehead region (Fig. 2). The bulk hair sample was divided following removal; half was submitted for radiocarbon analysis (see Chapter 2, pp. 43–47) and the other half was submitted for carbon and nitrogen isotope analysis. The second strand was cut into 1 cm sections along the strand from the point closest to the scalp down to the tip to enable an incremental study to be undertaken. It was not possible to take the hair root within the scalp due to conservation and aesthetic concerns and, as such, the very last growth immediately prior to death is not represented.

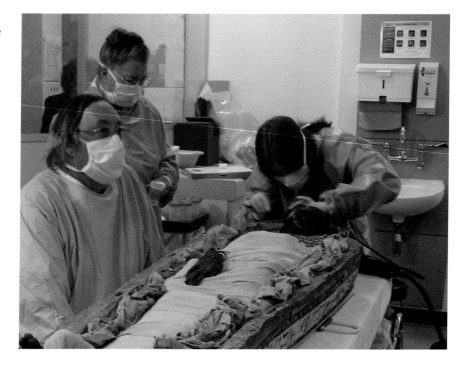

2 Samples of Takabuti's hair being taken in 2008 by Joanne Lowe, a conservator with National Museums Northern Ireland, assisted by Professor Rosalie David and John Denton, in the Manchester Royal Infirmary.
(photograph courtesy of Eileen Murphy, Queen's University Belfast)

As with samples for radiocarbon dating, those submitted for stable isotope analysis require cleaning beforehand to remove any external contamination that might affect the results. It was known that the ancient Egyptian embalmers applied a fat-based substance to Takabuti's hair and it was very important this was removed (see Chapter 2, pp. 62–63). Embalming unguents have an isotope signature of their own and, if left on the hair, the results would have been a mixture of both materials. Samples underwent an organic solvent pre-treatment followed by distilled water. They were then analysed on an Isotope Ratio Mass Spectrometer along with known value standards. The results are presented as δ (delta) values which is the offset from a standard multiplied by 1,000 for ease of interpretation.

Results

The results from the incremental isotope analysis show little variation across the six months leading up to Takabuti's death (Table 1). The $\delta^{13}C$ values are tightly clustered, with an average of -19.9‰. The $\delta^{13}C$ value for the bulk hair sample is also consistent with this result. This value is reflective of a diet based on temperate climate crops such as wheat and barley and is similar to $\delta^{13}C$ values obtained from other ancient Egyptian human hair samples (Fig. 3). Archaeological evidence supports the notion that ancient Egyptians preferentially grew and ate C3 crops, while their Nubian neighbours are known to have exploited both temperate and

Table 1 Stable isotope results from Takabuti's hair

Sample name	δ13C value (‰)	δ15N value (‰)	C:N ratio
TAK S1[1]	-19.8	13.5	3.9
TAK S2	-19.9	13.6	4.0
TAK S3	-19.9	13.6	4.0
TAK S4	-19.9	13.6	3.9
TAK S5	-19.9	13.6	4.0
TAK S6	-19.8	13.7	3.9
UBA-10090[2]	-19.9	13.7	4.0

[1] Hair increment taken from closest to scalp.
[2] Bulk hair sample also submitted for radiocarbon dating.

arid climate crops (C4), such as sorghum. This difference is reflected in δ13C values obtained from Nubian bulk and incremental hair analyses, which have produced δ13C values ranging from -11.7‰ (typical of C4 crops) to -19.5‰ (White 1993).

A recent isotope study by Touzeau et al. (2014) suggested that animal protein comprised 29 ± 19% of the ancient Egyptian diet. This was based on the study of δ13C values from hair samples with a range of -20.4‰ to -19.2‰. The δ13C values from Takabuti's hair fall within this range, suggesting that she consumed a similar quantity of animal protein.

The δ15N values are also tightly clustered, with an average of 13.6‰, while the bulk hair sample returned a very similar value of 13.7‰. These also lie within the range obtained from other ancient Egyptian hair samples. The δ15N values are slightly higher than expected for humans consuming largely C3 plants or the animals that consume these plants. This enrichment, as it is known, is possibly due to the aridity of the region, which places additional stresses on the body. The δ15N values from extremely arid regions, such as the Dakhleh and Kharga oases (White et al. 1995), for example, are higher than those exhibited by Takabuti. This affects our ability to determine the protein sources of Takabuti's diet using nitrogen isotopes, particularly with regard to identifying dairy and freshwater fish (Touzeau et al. 2014).

The C:N ratios are just outside of the acceptable range of 2.9 to 3.6 used to indicate well-preserved collagen (DeNiro 1985). This method is used primarily for determining the reliability of archaeological bone samples, but is conventionally applied to other tissues as well. This suggests that the hair may have undergone some post-mortem alteration or be affected by a source of contamination (see Chapter 2, pp. 58–64). The tight clustering of the results does not, however, support the

3 The bulk δ13C value from Takabuti's hair compared with average values from Middle Kingdom mummies (Macko et al. 1999), Late Period mummies from the Kharga Oasis (White et al. 1995) and mummies from Wadi Halfa, Nubia (White 1993). (prepared by Jenefer Metcalfe, University of Manchester)

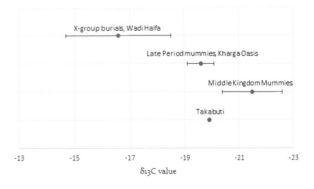

concern that embalming materials remained on the hair. These are often complex mixtures and, if accidentally included in the analysis, are likely to have produced more variable results across the series. Post-mortem degradation cannot be ruled out, however, and the isotope data must be considered with caution despite falling within the ranges expected.

Conclusions

Both the $\delta^{13}C$ values and the $\delta^{15}N$ values suggest that Takabuti's diet remained stable over the six months prior to her death. There is no evidence of a change in the source of dietary protein caused by seasonal changes, movement or illness. The isotope values are consistent with other hair analyses from ancient Egypt and the conclusions drawn from the large number of archaeological bone samples studied. They are suggestive of the consumption of a largely C3 plant-based diet in the region, along with the consumption of some animal protein. The isotope data suggests that Takabuti's diet was similar to that of other human individuals from ancient Egypt who have been studied using this method. The hair had undergone some degradation, however, and the implications of this for the isotope results are difficult to determine, so the conclusions must remain tentative.

References

DeNiro, M. J. 1985. Postmortem preservation and alteration of in vivo bone collagen isotope ratios in relation to palaeodietary reconstruction. *Nature* 317, 806–09.

Katzenberg, M. A. 2000. Stable isotope analysis: a tool for studying past diet, demography and life history. In M. A. Katzenberg (ed.), *The Biological Anthropology of the Human Skeleton*, pp. 305–27. New York: Wiley.

Macko, S. A., Engel, M. H., Andrusevich, V., Lubec, G., O'Connell, T. C. and Hedges, R. E. M. 1999. Documenting diet in ancient human populations through stable isotope analysis of hair. *Philosophical Transactions of the Royal Society of London, Series B* 354, 65–76.

Schulting, R. J. 1998. Slighting the sea: stable isotope evidence for the transition to farming in northwestern Europe. *Documenta Praehistorica* 25, 203–18.

Touzeau, A., Amiot, R., Blichert-Toft, J., Flandrois, J.-P., Fourel, F., Grossi, V., Martineau, F., Richardin, P. and Lécuyer, C. 2014. Diet of ancient Egyptians inferred from stable isotope systematics. *Journal of Archaeological Science* 46, 114–24.

White, C. D. 1993. Isotopic determination of seasonality in diet and death from Nubian mummy hair. *Journal of Archaeological Science* 20, 657–66.

White, C. D., Longstaffe, F. and Law, K. 1995. Isotopic analysis of hair and skin from Kharga Oasis mummies. Unpublished report to the American Museum of Natural History.

4

Takabuti's Death and Mummification

How Did Takabuti Die?

Robert Loynes

When analysing and researching ancient Egyptian mummies, one of the frequent expectations (or at least hopes) is of finding a cause of death. Unfortunately, in most cases this hope is not satisfied. The reason is that the very act of mummification/embalming often involves the removal of the organs of the trunk and skull. Even if the trunk organs are treated (i.e. desiccated) and returned to the body, they are usually distorted to such an extent as to make the diagnosis of pathology impossible. The soft tissue structures of the body wall and limbs are also usually very distorted by the process of desiccation. The end result is that the skeleton is the only part of the body left relatively undisturbed by the mummification techniques. Unfortunately, many disease processes, and particularly those causing death, do not leave any 'marker' or 'signature' within the skeletal tissues. The exceptions are skeletal congenital anomalies, trauma, infection, and primary and secondary malignant bone disease.

Analysis of the CT scan of Takabuti's body revealed that she had died as a young woman in her late 20s or early 30s (see Chapter 3, p. 67). No evidence of ongoing illness was evident in her skeleton or found in the samples of mummified tissue analysed using proteomics (see Chapter 3, p. 81). Although not as long-lived as modern populations, ancient Egyptians often survived until middle age, and this implies an early death in the case of Takabuti that requires some explanation.

Weapon Trauma

Clear evidence of injury was evident in the chest of Takabuti. From the CT scan a feature in the upper left side of the chest is clearly apparent.

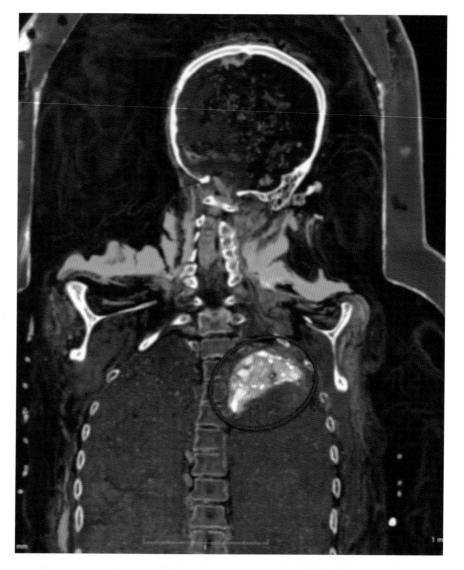

1 Coronal view of the chest showing the pack in the left upper thorax. The pack appears to have been made from resin-soaked linen. Note the resin collar at the neck area.
(© R. D. Loynes and the University of Manchester)

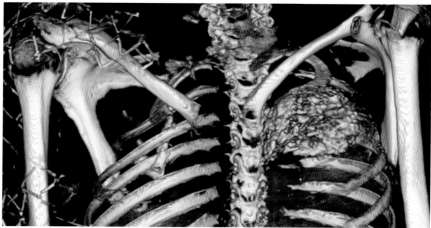

2 3D reconstruction of the thorax showing the pack.
(© R. D. Loynes and the University of Manchester)

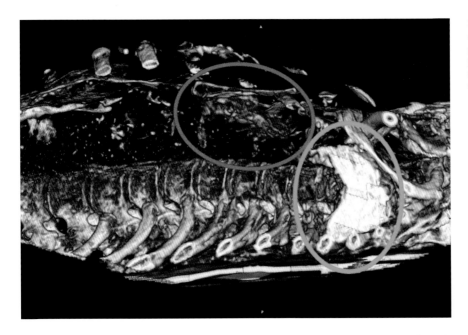

3 A para-sagittal section of the thorax showing the pack (green ellipse) and the heart package (blue ellipse). (© R. D. Loynes and the University of Manchester)

This is in the form of a pack, probably formed by linen infiltrated with resin (Figs. 1–3). It should also be noted that the rib cage was normal in shape and no evidence of distortion by compression, a situation often present in Roman Period mummies, was observed.

On inspection of the anatomy of the ribs on the left, it rapidly became apparent that there is damage to the second, third, fourth, fifth and sixth ribs in the region of their necks – in other words posteriorly. Although the second and sixth ribs exhibit fractures, there is a clear loss of some

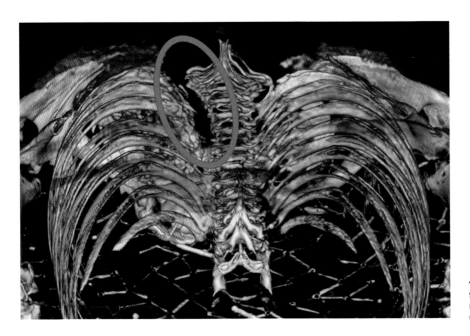

4 3D reconstruction of the thorax showing the rib injuries. (© R. D. Loynes and the University of Manchester)

of the rib substance posteriorly in the other ribs (Fig. 4). Furthermore, a fracture of the medial edge of the left scapula is also evident. While this area is no longer in the proximity of the rib fractures, it is quite feasible that the scapula lay more medially during life. Therefore, it is distinctly possible that the left rib and scapula injuries were inflicted at the same time.

Addressing the rib injuries in more detail, it must be noted that this area of the trunk is covered by relatively bulky muscle groups – the erector spinae muscles. The overlying protection from these muscles means that the posterior ends of the ribs are rarely damaged by blunt trauma in life. It follows that only a sharp-edged weapon thrust with force into this area through the tissues and from behind an individual could have resulted in a broader area of damage at the level of the ribs as a result of energy transmission, causing splintering of the ribs. The defects caused by the rib fractures and missing parts of ribs are approximately 6.5–7 cm in length and 2.5 cm at the widest part of the defect (due to loss of rib substance).

As stated above, the injuries in the left side of the thoracic cavity were associated with a pack which appears to have been inserted by the embalmers. Whether this was a mechanical pack to close the wound or was a more symbolic item like a poultice to magically induce healing is open to debate. The use of poultices to heal wounds is well described in the *Edwin Smith Papyrus* – Cases 40 and 41 (Breasted 1991). The concept of a 'whole', 'uncorrupted' body for use in the afterlife (one that has been 'healed') is ensured by Spell 154 of the *Book of the Dead* (Taylor 2010). It is clear that the linen pack was inserted prior to the addition of the granular material that was used to pack the thoracic and abdominal cavities during mummification (see Chapter 4, pp. 108–10).

A wound in this region delivered with sufficient force to damage five ribs to this extent would have caused a serious chest injury. This could easily have resulted in damage to the internal structures of the upper thoracic cavity, namely the great vessels, aorta, the left lung and its enclosing pleura. The end result, from a pathological point of view, would have been a traumatic haemo-pneumothorax – a collapsed lung with associated catastrophic bleeding. Even today this would be a challenging situation for doctors to attempt to treat, and in Takabuti's time it would, inevitably, have resulted in a rapid death.

In the absence of an attested witness statement of the event, absolute certainty cannot be reached, but these explanations for the observed wound in Takabuti's chest are far and away the most plausible. As to the manner in which the injuries were inflicted, the blow was clearly delivered from behind and with significant force. A weapon capable of causing a wound of these dimensions would have required a blade with a sharp edge at least 7–7.5 cm in length. Weapons available in Egypt during the 25th Dynasty that could have inflicted such a wound are discussed elsewhere in this chapter (see pp. 96–99).

Conclusion

The possibility that Takabuti sustained these injuries accidentally requires some consideration. However, the chances of accidentally falling backwards against a sufficiently sharp object with enough force to penetrate the chest wall and fracture five ribs as well as the shoulder blade are vanishingly small. Therefore, the conclusion must be that this was a case of deliberate wounding and that Takabuti was murdered.

References

Breasted, J. H. 1991. *The Edwin Smith Surgical Papyrus, Volume 2: Facsimile Plates and Line for Line Hieroglyphic Transliteration.* Chicago: Oriental Institute Publications.

Taylor, J. H. 2010. *Journey Through the Afterlife: Ancient Egyptian Book of the Dead.* London: British Museum.

Weapons Possibly Involved in Takabuti's Murder
Rosalie David

This section includes an attempt to identify the weapon used to inflict the penetrating chest injury found in Takabuti's mummy (see Chapter 4, pp. 91–95), in the hope that this might throw some light on the circumstances of the attack. Was Takabuti the victim of violence within her family, or was the wound inflicted by soldiers, perhaps when the Assyrians laid siege to Thebes, or during other times of local unrest and conflict that continued throughout the 25th Dynasty?

The Egyptians developed almost all their military weapons from those used since the earliest times for hunting (c. 4000 BC). The oldest cutting and stabbing weapons were made of flint and stone but, by c. 3200 BC, these materials were partly replaced by copper from the Eastern Desert and Sinai. The production of

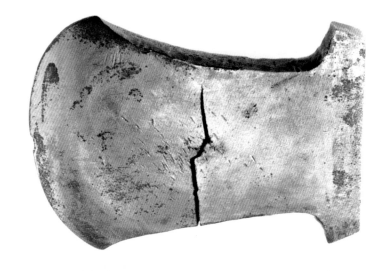

1 Bronze axe and the pottery mould in which it was made, from the pyramid workmen's town of Kahun, Egypt, c. 1890 BC.
(courtesy of Manchester Museum, University of Manchester)

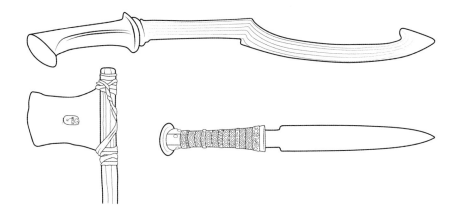

2 Examples of weapons used in the Egyptian army: a dagger, axe and *kepesh* (sickle sword). New Kingdom – Late Period (c. 1569–656 BC).
(drawn by Libby Mulqueeny, Queen's University Belfast, after Partridge 2002: figs. 28, 70, 78 and 80)

bronze (an alloy of copper and tin) probably originated in Mesopotamia, and at some point it was introduced into Egypt. Although the date of its arrival there is uncertain, some bronze tools and weapons can be firmly dated to the 12th Dynasty (1991–1786 BC). These demonstrate the technology involved in casting tools and weapons in pottery moulds (Fig. 1). However, metal-smelting techniques only developed slowly, and for many centuries flint blades were used alongside those manufactured in copper or bronze. This was because flint was more accessible and produced sharper blades. Stone also continued to be used for other weapons, such as maces.

The introduction of iron weapons changed the whole perspective of warfare. Large-scale smelting production started in Asia, but Egypt only established an ironworking industry at Naucratis in the sixth century BC. The Assyrians, without their own iron resources, accessed supplies from their subjugated neighbours, and initiated the use of iron weapons. This gave their armies a considerable advantage over those, including the Egyptians, who were still fighting with bronze weapons. Iron was a much better alternative because its ore was cheaper than others and more widely available; iron weapons were also stronger, and the superior sharpness of their edges could be retained for longer.

The range of weapons employed by the Egyptian army was very similar to those of neighbouring countries. Egyptian examples that might have been used to inflict Takabuti's fatal injury include knives, daggers, axes and the *kepesh* (sickle sword) (Fig. 2). The Assyrian infantry was armed with long, double-headed spears incorporating iron spearheads, and short iron swords and daggers. All knives and daggers were used in close combat to stab an opponent, whereas the *kepesh*, with its long, curved blade, was designed as a slashing weapon. Egyptian axes, which incorporated semi-circular metal blades lashed to wooden handles, had considerable capacity to deliver a serious penetrative wound.

Physical evidence from Takabuti's mummy provides some indication of the type of weapon that was used, although it is difficult to be absolutely definitive because the morphology of the wound has been significantly distorted by the mummification procedures, and by desiccation of the tissues. Additionally, other relevant information – such as the relative positions of the assailant and victim (perhaps influenced by relative height) and the victim's posture – cannot be definitively determined. However, it can be concluded from the shape of the wound that the cutting edge of the weapon was at least 7–7.5 cm (3 inches) in length (see Chapter 4, pp. 94–95). It appears that the blade was probably thrust deep into the ribs at the centre of the wound from behind. Here, missing fragments indicate that the ribs were shattered. This makes it a more likely point of entry than either end of the wound where the ribs, although fractured, remain intact.

The length of the blade is difficult to determine, but since the rib wound is at least 7–7.5 cm in length, and the blade had to penetrate soft tissues to reach the ribs, the blade of the weapon could have measured up to around 10 cm (4 inches). The rib damage suggests that the wound was probably inflicted by a weapon with a slightly convex edge.

Some weapons can be eliminated because they do not fit with this evidence. For example, although the *kepesh* has a curved blade, its point is not sharp, and it was used for slashing rather than stabbing. Knives and daggers were widely used by the Egyptians, and some of the Assyrian daggers have leaf-shaped or curved blades.

As stated above, the fatal weapon apparently had a blade of around 10 cm with a slightly convex edge. The wound in the ribs is symmetrical, indicating that the width of the blade's cutting edge was around 7 cm. A stabbing action

3 Wall-scene showing a line of soldiers: four carry axes, and (far right) a *kepesh* (sickle sword) is visible in the hand of a man out of view. Temple of Hatshepsut at Deir el-Bahri, Egypt, reign of Tuthmosis III (1504–1482 BC).
(photograph courtesy of Keith White, University of Manchester)

with a knife or dagger would leave an asymmetrical wound if it was 'dragged' downwards from the second to the sixth rib. Therefore, the most likely candidate is the axe (Fig. 3). Such a weapon has the weight and power to deliver a swinging, devastating blow generally capable of penetrating armour and breaking bones. In the attack on Takabuti, an axe with a fairly short and slightly convex edge could have impacted on the central ribs and then caused the adjacent shattering.

The physical evidence suggests that Takabuti was attacked from behind (not vertically from above, as this would have produced a more tapered wound). A likely scenario is that her assailant, holding an axe, chased after her, with arms bent rather than in a straight position. This would have given the weapon its maximum force to deliver the fatal blow.

Although we can only speculate about the exact circumstances of Takabuti's brutal death, the strong probability that an axe was used to kill her does indicate that she might have met her death during one of the armed conflicts that beset the Theban population during her lifetime. However, there is nothing to suggest that an Assyrian, rather than an Egyptian, assailant was involved. Over the millennia, the axe became a key weapon for the Egyptian army, and she may have fallen victim to one of her own people.

Reference
Partridge, R. B. 2002. *Fighting Pharaohs: Weapons and Warfare in Ancient Egypt.* Manchester: Peartree Publishing.

Mummification Methods Used on Takabuti

Robert Loynes and Judith Adams†

Although Egyptian mummies from the Predynastic and Byzantine (or Coptic) periods were natural mummies, those from other eras were usually anthropogenic in type. That is, a specific set of processes was used to preserve the body of the deceased for use in the afterlife.

The contemporary records from ancient Egypt do not contain many details of how mummification/embalming was performed. Limited archaeological evidence – the so-called embalmers' caches – provides some information about the embalming process. An inscribed text known as the *Embalming Ritual* adds other details from the Roman Period. However, our main source of knowledge about the procedure remains the account written by Herodotus in Book 2 of his *Histories*. This is based on information given to him by Egyptian priests and scribes in the mid-fifth century BC. He described the mummification process as consisting essentially of three parts – excerebration, evisceration and desiccation (David 2002; Sélincourt and Burn 1972). While this description relates to the Late Period, Egyptologists use it as a benchmark against which to compare and contrast the many variations found in the mummification process. Scientific studies of mummification indicate that techniques varied from era to era and that the many embalming workshops added their own variations to the general practice current at the time (Loynes 2015). Herodotus describes how relatives of the deceased had a choice of procedures of different costs as mummification became more widely available.

Takabuti's Mummification

The Head and Neck

In the case of Takabuti (thought to have lived in the 25th Dynasty), the mummification techniques used included excerebration, evisceration, desiccation, packing of the cavities and subsequent wrapping (bandaging). However, detailed analysis of Takabuti's CT scans reveals significant variations from the common practices of embalming.

Commencing with the head, the images show that the brain was removed (although a little cerebral tissue remains). However, excerebration did not take place via the usual trans-nasal route which would have involved removal of the brain through the nasal cavity, with perforation of the nasal air sinuses in either the ethmoid or sphenoid bones or both. In Takabuti's case, access to the cranial cavity was achieved via the foramen magnum at the base of the skull. To accomplish this, it would have been necessary to divide all the muscles at the junction of the head and neck posteriorly and on both sides. This allows the head to be flexed forwards (and possibly rotated to the side) thereby providing access to the foramen magnum. Following removal of most of the cerebral tissue, foreign material was introduced into the cranium. The scan images indicate that at least two different types of material were used, as assessed by Hounsfield numbers – a measure of radio-density (Hounsfield 1980). Although it was difficult to identify these materials, one appears to have been introduced in liquid form, thereby producing a 'fluid level', which was followed by the insertion of granular material. A substance introduced in liquid form which then sets is often identified as resin, but in the case of Takabuti, the X-ray density of this intra-cranial material differs from the definite resin (confirmed by chemical analysis) found around her neck (see Chapter 4, pp. 107–108). It follows, therefore, that the intra-cranial substance is either not resin or consists of resin combined with some other material.

Use of the trans-foraminal route is uncommon and usually results in permanent disruption of the area between the base of the skull and cervical vertebrae. However, Takabuti's anatomy was restored to normal and the alignment preserved by using resin as a firm neck collar. This technique has been found in only two other cases by one of the authors (RL) in a series of over 100 CT scans of Egyptian mummies (Fig. 1).

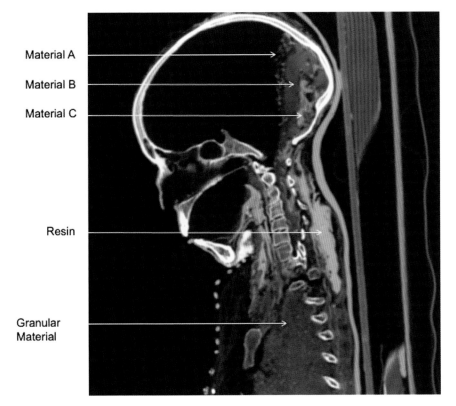

Material A

Material B

Material C

Resin

Granular
Material

1 Takabuti's head and neck showing intra-cranial material and resin around the neck.
(© R. D. Loynes and the University of Manchester)

The eyes were treated by incising the eyeballs, removing the vitreous body and lens and then packing with linen to preserve the spherical shape. The difference between packing the orbit and packing the globe of the eye is distinguished by the presence of remnants of the optic nerve and orbital muscles, which are retained along with the globe of the eye.

Examination of the oral cavity revealed that the tongue had been compressed towards the back of the mouth. Although there is no evidence of material within the mouth, the empty cavity is indicative that it would have been packed with material during mummification, which has been subsequently removed and lost. This may have happened during the unwrapping of 1835, although there is no mention of this in contemporary accounts (see Chapter 1, pp. 30–37).

The Trunk

The absence of any sign of organs indicates a complete and thorough evisceration. While there was no evidence of residual viscera or canopic packages, a bundle was located within the anterior part of the upper thorax. Within this package, which is clearly wrapped in linen, is a structure which contains cavities very close in appearance to the ventricles of the heart (Fig. 2). Structures within the tissue mass – almost certainly the ascending segment, arch and descending segment of the aorta – are also present. Although the soft tissues within the package have been distorted to an extent, the appearance of a heart

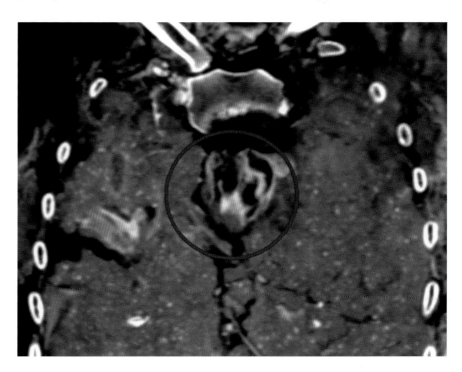

2 Coronal view of the chest showing the package containing the heart.
(© R. D. Loynes and the University of Manchester)

is undeniable. Egyptologists generally expect the heart to have been retained during mummification, as it was required for the 'weighing of the heart' ceremony on the Day of Judgement. However, in over 100 CT scans of Egyptian mummies examined by one of the authors (RL), only 25% were found to contain a heart, a finding that has also been confirmed by other workers (Wade and Nelson 2013). In only two of these was the heart contained in a wrapped package, as opposed to remaining within the chest without any attempt at extraction. Again, Takabuti's mummification is unusual in this regard.

The method of evisceration used in the mummy of Takabuti is difficult to ascertain with certainty as the anterior abdominal wall was severely damaged during the unwrapping in 1835. However, there is a hint that a left flank incision was used in one of the remaining fragments of tissue where possible edges are evident (Fig. 3). Furthermore, the CT scan indicates that a perineal (pelvic floor) route was also used during evisceration (Fig. 4). Once more this is an unusual, although well described (Wade and Nelson 2013), route used by embalmers in ancient Egypt. One feature that supports the hypothesis of an additional left flank incision is the fact that complete evisceration had occurred, this being rarely, if ever, achieved via an exclusively perineal route.

Following complete evisceration, the body cavity was solidly packed with a granular material. Four points are notable about this packing. First, it almost certainly completely filled the whole cavity, although in most cases any packing introduced only partly filled the cavity. Secondly, during the unwrapping of 1835 an aromatic aroma was noticed. This fits well with the statement by Herodotus about the use of 'an infusion of

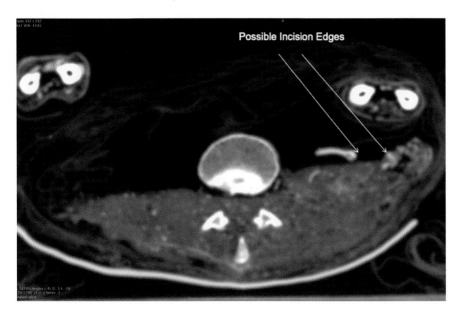

3 Fragment of Takabuti's abdominal wall showing evidence of a possible flank incision.
(© R. D. Loynes and the University of Manchester)

4 Sagittal section of the trunk showing perineal evisceration and subsequent disruption of the resin seal as a result of pressure from above (red ellipse).
(© R. D. Loynes and the University of Manchester)

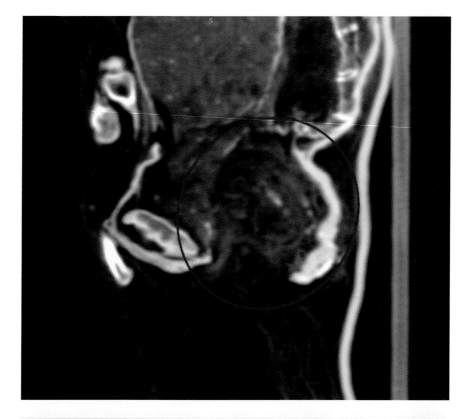

5 Strong pressure from the granular packing (green arrow) has caused the perineal packing, which had been introduced from below (dotted red lines), to rotate backwards (yellow arrow) resulting in the separation and rotation of the resin seal.
(© R. D. Loynes and the University of Manchester)

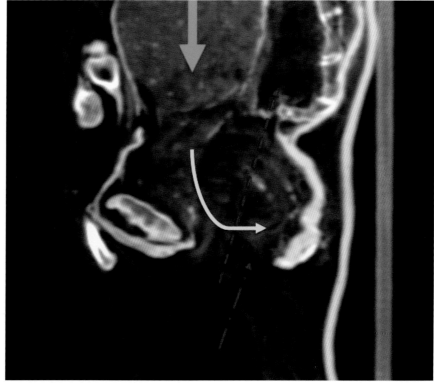

pounded spices. After that it is filled with pure bruised myrrh, cassia and every other aromatic substance with the exception of frankincense' (Sélincourt and Burn 1972, pp. 160–61). Thirdly, the work of Counsell (2016) also confirms that the use of aromatic substances in preparing the body is responsible for the distinctive, spicy smell associated with many mummies. Finally, samples of the packing material from within Takabuti were analysed as part of the current study and the results indicated that it contained sawdust largely derived from cedar mixed with resin (see Chapter 4, pp. 108–10).

Analysis of the perineum indicates that, prior to wrapping, linen was introduced upwards into the pelvic cavity and the defect sealed with resin. Following this, however, the granular material was packed in so tightly from above, and with such intensity, that the pelvic packing was forced downwards and posteriorly, thereby disrupting the resin casing (Fig. 5).

The Limbs
Disruption of the left fingers, with separation of the phalanges from the metacarpals, is evident (Fig. 6). In addition, the loss of several of the phalanges of the left fingers has occurred. It was previously suggested

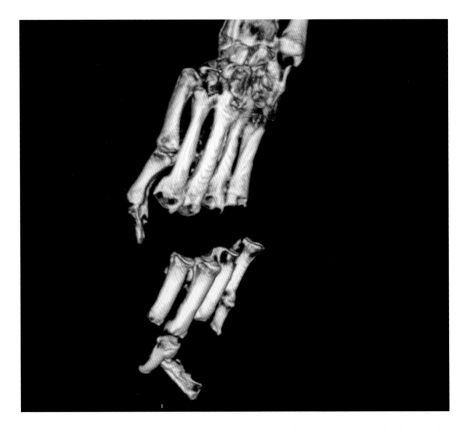

6 3D reconstruction of the left hand showing the separation of the fingers and loss of some phalanges which have subsequently been identified located within the granular packing material of the thorax.
(© R. D. Loynes and the University of Manchester)

during the 2008 study that this could perhaps have arisen at the time of unwrapping in 1835. However, this cannot be the case as two of the missing phalanges were found deep within the packing material in the thoracic cavity. This finding indicates that these bones were separated from the hand before the mummification process had been completed.

Conclusions

With the possible exception of the left hand, all of the soft tissues of the body wall and limbs in Takabuti's body have been well preserved. This indicates that the mummification process was successful and involved effective desiccation and the subsequent application of unguents.

A number of the techniques of mummification evident in Takabuti are unusual, particularly the trans-foraminal excerebration, with restoration of the anatomy in the atlanto-occipital region (junction of head and neck), followed by the introduction of at least two types of foreign material into the cranium. Evisceration was complete and, with the exception of the packaged heart, none of the other organs was returned to the interior of the body. The evisceration routes almost certainly comprised a combination of a left flank incision with an added perineal approach, following which the body cavity was tightly packed with a granular substance, recently shown to consist of a mixture of sawdust, largely derived from cedar, and resin (see Chapter 4, pp. 108–10). The application of several unusual techniques of mummification might well be a reflection of Takabuti's relatively high status in the society of her era.

References

Counsell, D. 2016. *Mummies, Magic and Medicine in Ancient Egypt.* Manchester: Manchester University Press.

David, A. R. 2002. *Religion and Magic in Ancient Egypt.* London: Penguin.

Hounsfield, G. N. 1980. Computed medical imaging. Nobel Lecture 8 December 1979. *Journal of Radiology* 61, 6–7.

Loynes, R. 2015. *Prepared for Eternity: A Study of Human Embalming Techniques in Ancient Egypt Using Computerised Tomography Scans of Mummies.* Oxford: Archaeopress.

Sélincourt, A. de, and Burn, A. R. 1972. *Herodotus: The Histories.* Rev. edn. Harmondsworth: Penguin.

Wade, A. D. and Nelson, A. J. 2013. Radiological evaluation of the evisceration tradition in ancient Egyptian mummies. *HOMO – Journal of Comparative Human Biology* 64, 1–28.

Analysis of Takabuti's Mummification Resin and Packing Material

Keith White, Bart van Dongen and Sharon Fraser

Lipid analyses by gas chromatography mass spectrometry (GCMS; Fig. 1A) of the mummification resin obtained from Takabuti's neck area indicates a dominance of lipids of plant and/or animal origin. This includes contributions from animal fats or from the breakdown of the mummy tissues themselves (Brockbals et al. 2018), and a series of compounds probably derived from the dehydration of pine resin, most notably a series of dehydroabietic acids (Łucejko et al. 2017; Brockbals et al. 2018) that occur in a number of pine trees. One specific acid observed was ricinoleic acid, obtained from the seeds of the castor oil plant *Ricinus communis L.*, which has been identified in other Egyptian mummy samples (Łucejko et al. 2017) and indicates the use of castor oil during the embalming process. Lipid analyses revealed the absence of natural petroleum markers, suggesting that bitumen was not used during the embalming process.

These findings were supported by thermal-desorption and pyrolysis-GC-MS analyses which also indicate a dominance of material of plant and/or animal origin (Figs. 1B and 1C), including camphor and retene. The latter is the final stable thermal degradation product of pine (Pinaceae) resin tars (Łucejko et al. 2017), thereby supporting the presence of dehydroabietic acids and pine resin observed in the lipid analyses. Camphor can be derived from different plant oils, including cedar oil, but cannot be linked to a specific source (Łucejko et al. 2017). Once again, no evidence for the presence of bitumen could be detected, which supports the assertion that it was not used during Takabuti's embalming process. Altogether, the different analyses indicate that the resinous material found on Takabuti is comparable to that observed in other Egyptian mummies and includes the presence of fats, oils or waxes, of both plant and animal origin, with contributions from pine and castor oil as well as a lack of bitumen.

Previous examinations of mummies dating from the Predynastic to the Roman Period indicate that bitumen was not used before the New Kingdom. However, such studies have revealed that bitumen was used in the mummification of 50% of individuals from the New Kingdom to Late Period, increasing to 87% during the Ptolemaic and Roman eras. There may have been theological reasons for the increased use of bitumen in mummification. Bitumen would colour the mummy black, which was associated with regeneration and Osiris, the god of the afterlife. The greater availability of bitumen due to increased trade was another likely reason. Bitumen probably also reduced the rate of decay, including in

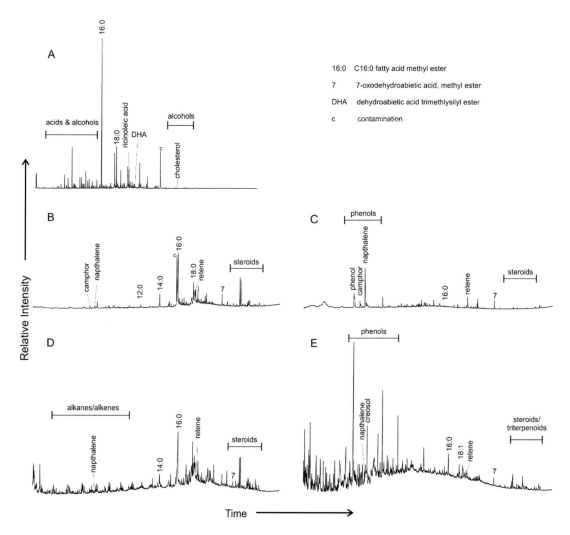

those individuals that were not eviscerated. As Takabuti was eviscerated, however, perhaps the use of bitumen was not thought necessary (see Chapter 4, pp. 103–105).

Various inert packing materials have been previously recorded in ancient Egyptian mummies, including sand, soil and small wood shavings (sawdust). Light and scanning electron microscopy (Fig. 2) revealed that the packing material from the mummy of Takabuti is largely composed of small (~0.5–<0.1mm) wood shavings and sawdust (Figs. 3A and 3B). Unidentified plant remains, possibly stems, were also noted. Earlier researchers noted the presence of sawdust in a number of ancient Egyptian mummies examined from the nineteenth and early twentieth centuries to the present (see Amorós and Vozenin-Serra 1998). Sawdust appears to be particularly prevalent in the packing material of mummies from the latter part of the Third Intermediate Period, and also

2 Dr Keith White and Dr Lewis Hughes examining the packing material from Takabuti using a scanning electron microscope in the Williamson Research Centre, University of Manchester. The wood particles that constitute the bulk of the packing material can be seen on the bottom right monitor. The machine also detects X-rays generated when the electron beam that produces the image strikes the sample. Each element releases X-rays of different energies, and so it was possible to identify the elements, and their relative amounts, in the packing material.
(© University of Manchester)

from the Late Period. The larger wood shavings in Takabuti's packing material revealed numerous longitudinal vessels called tracheids (see Fig. 3B) that transport water and mineral salts. The flakes consist almost entirely of these vessels which is a characteristic of softwood rather than hardwood, which have numerous cell types. High magnification scanning electron microscope images revealed inter-vessel pits (see Fig. 3B, arrows) on the cell wall which connect the tracheids with other cells. The shape and appearance of these pits are diagnostic of softwoods, and those in our samples are characteristic of cedar wood, probably cedar of Lebanon (*Cedrus libani*). Some other, probably local, softwoods were also present, but the fragments were too small to identify. Many authors have suggested that the sawdust was derived from cedar wood on the basis of smell and the embalming procedures described by Classical authors such as Herodotus in Book 2 of his *Histories* (Sélincourt and Burn 1972: 86–88). Cedar wood was also found in the abdominal cavity of the mummy of Namenkh-Amon, who lived between the 24th and 30th Dynasties (Amorós and Vozenin-Serra 1998).

Numerous small, hard, irregularly shaped darker aggregates were also common in Takabuti's packing material (see Fig. 3A, arrows). Although superficially having the appearance of sand (see Fig. 3B), X-ray spectroscopy revealed the aggregates to have a similar X-ray energy profile to the wood shavings. Sand would generate X-rays more characteristic of silicon and calcium, and the similarity to wood indicates that the aggregates are also organic. Therefore thermal desorption and pyrolysis-GCMS analysis of the packing material was undertaken. The analysis indicated a dominance of wood (lignin) origin, including phenolic type structures, in line with the presence of the wood shavings (see Figs. 1D and 1E). Also present was a substantial contribution of material of plant and/

 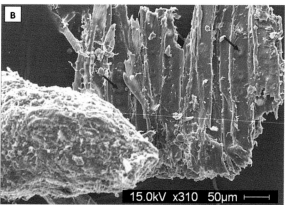

1 mm

15.0kV x310 50µm

3A Dark-field light micrograph of packing material showing particles and flakes of wood (<0.1 to 3 mm; red arrows) plus darker-coloured aggregates of variable shape and size (~0.1 to 2 mm; blue arrows).
3B High magnification scanning electron micrograph of packing material showing an elongated aggregate (left) and a wood shaving (centre and right). The red arrows show the inter-vessel bordered pits on the cell wall connecting the elongate tracheid vessels with other cells.
(images courtesy of Keith White, University of Manchester)

or animal origin, comparable to that observed in the resinous material from the wrappings, suggesting a similar origin for both the mummification and packing material resins. Once again, no evidence for the use of bitumen was observed. Amorós and Vozenin-Serra (1998) also recorded unidentified resinous material in the abdominal cavity of the mummy of Namenkh-Amon. It is here suggested that the resin was added in liquid form to impart a pleasant odour to the packing material and, hence, to the mummy.

We suggest that the wood shavings and dust used in the packing material were from the workshops engaged in the production of coffins and tomb goods. If so, this indicates a possibly close commercial relationship between the funerary workshops and those engaged in mummification.

References

Amorós, V. A. and Vozenin-Serra, C. 1998. New evidence for the use of cedar sawdust for embalming by ancient Egyptians. *The Journal of Egyptian Archaeology* 84, 228–31.

Brockbals, L., Habicht, M., Hajdas, I., Galassi, F. M., Rühli, F. J. and Kraemer, T. 2018. Untargeted metabolomics-like screening approach for chemical characterization and differentiation of canopic jar and mummy samples from ancient Egypt using GC-high resolution MS. *Analyst* 143, 4503–12.

Clark, K. A., Ikram, S. and Evershed, R. P. 2016. The significance of petroleum bitumen in ancient Egyptian mummies. *Philosophical Transactions of the Royal Society A: Mathematical, Physical and Engineering Sciences* 374, 20160229.

Łucejko, J., Connan, J., Orsini, S., Ribechini, E. and Modugno, F., 2017. Chemical analyses of Egyptian mummification balms and organic residues from storage jars dated from the Old Kingdom to the Copto-Byzantine period. *Journal of Archaeological Science* 85, 1–12.

Sélincourt, A. de, and Burn, A. R. 1972. *Herodotus: The Histories*. Rev. edn. Harmondsworth: Penguin.

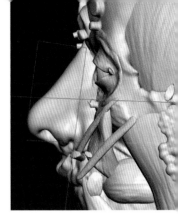

5

Takabuti Revealed

The Face of Takabuti
Caroline Wilkinson and Sarah Shrimpton

Introduction to Facial Reconstruction, Depiction and Cognitive Bias

The human face is critical to social interaction, personal resilience and population hierarchy, and its influence on status, power and success is well established in psychology literature. The face embodies identity, and our judgements about people from the past may, in part, be in response to the visualisation of facial appearance. Facial depiction can stimulate a museum audience to engage with archaeological remains as human rather than as objects/artefacts, and the recreation of personal identity can be pivotal in the social interpretation of those remains. A facial depiction creates empathy between the audience and the individual (Buti et al. 2017), and helps to 'bring the person to life'.

Facial reconstruction is the process used to reconstruct the shape of the face and features based on the interpretation of skeletal and/or preserved soft tissues. The addition of textures to this face shape (e.g. hair, eye and skin colour, and surface detail) provides the final facial depiction. This technique can also be used to assist in forensic investigation, where the facial reconstruction of unidentified remains may elicit leads from the public. Over the last half century there have been a large number of historical and archaeological facial depictions, such as those of Richard III, Philip II of Macedonia and Robert the Bruce. In addition, facial depictions have been exhibited for preserved human remains, such as bog bodies, ice mummies and ancient Egyptians. Facial depictions of Egyptian mummies prove popular with the public, and this is thought to be related to the human need to restore personhood to human remains.

Existing research has established and reported on the relationship between the hard (skull) and soft (flesh) tissues, providing guidelines on how to predict and reconstruct the face either manually or using a computerised system (Wilkinson 2010). While this research suggests good levels of accuracy in relation to the prediction of facial morphology, the addition of colour and surface detail is notoriously unreliable, and how these choices are made in relation to facial depiction can have a very strong effect on the appearance and perceived accuracy/resemblance. There is a greater likelihood at this point that stereotypes could bias the end result. Subjective opinion is always conditioned by context, and facial depictions can affect the course of scientific research by contributing to and perpetuating confirmation bias. In fact, facial depictions play an active part in academic debate and construct much of the knowledge that the public has of people from the past. Archaeological facial depictions can therefore provide museums with a means of visualising the past.

Facial depictions of ancient populations may perpetuate confirmation bias relating to gender and ancestry. For example, female subjects are more frequently depicted with passive, indirect gazes, while male subjects are more likely to be shown with direct gazes and aggressive expressions. In addition, facial depictions may, often unintentionally, reinforce the concept of biological race and popular notions of racial identity by adhering to the traditional model of cranial typology. Since human skulls do not indicate skin tone or hairstyle, practitioners will tend to include these features based on racial or cultural stereotypes. Many historical depictions have been contentious in the choice of skin colour and the visualisation of ethnicity, with controversial subjects including ancient Egyptian mummies, early ancestors and famous historical figures. This is, in part, a result of the audience expectation for realistic and high-quality models for exposition, forcing decisions relating to skin colour, even when there is little justification for the choice. The degree of realism may therefore be influenced by the potential for display and the interests of the museum visitor.

There has been a great deal of discussion relating to the depiction of ancient Egyptians, and racial readings of ancient Egyptian faces remain significant. Assumptions concerning the appearance of ancient people based on modern human appearance may be erroneous, as the genetic pairings of features today may not have always been fixed. This is evidenced by the two depictions of Cheddar Man some 20 years apart, the original demonstrating assumptions of pale skin and dark hair/eyes, and the more recent supported by ancient DNA analysis identifying genetic markers of dark skin pigmentation and pale-coloured eyes (Brace et al. 2019). Forensic DNA phenotyping refers to the prediction of appearance traits directly from biological materials, and the externally visible characteristics that involve pigmentation (iris, head hair, skin) are currently the only examples of practical forensic DNA phenotyping. Where an investigation includes DNA analysis these details can be utilised for the facial depiction, but even they will not provide the whole picture when it comes to living appearance. Where a DNA profile is not available, some museums have chosen to depict faces from the past in greyscale rather than colour (see Swaney and Balachandran 2018) in an attempt to limit confirmation bias and to explicitly expose the lack of evidence for skin, eye and hair colour.

Depicting the Face of Takabuti

A facial depiction of Takabuti was produced in 2008 for the BBC Northern Ireland television programme *Show Me the Mummy: The Face of Takabuti* and the exhibition at the Ulster Museum, to complement the other elements of the ancient Egyptian display and to facilitate a human connection between the audience and the mummified remains. An entirely digital workflow, from CT scan to finished facial depiction, was achieved. Starting with a 3D model of the skull (Fig. 1), the updated and

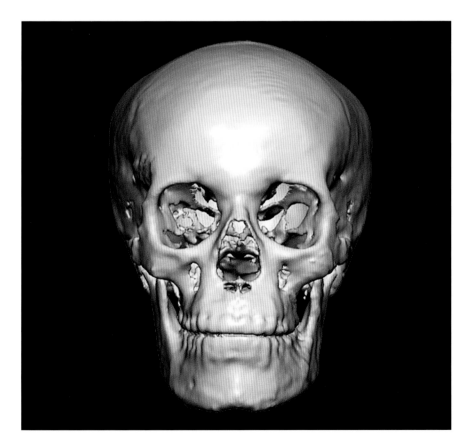

1 A visualisation of the digital skull model of Takabuti, extracted from the CT scan and shown in 3D Systems Freeform software.
(image courtesy of Face Lab at Liverpool John Moores University)

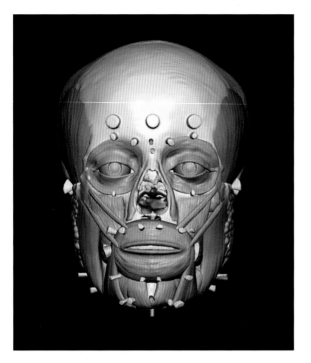

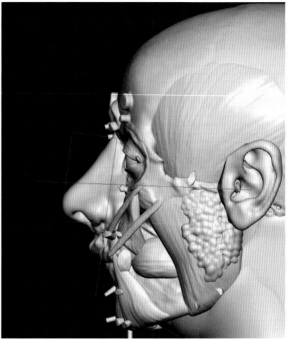

2 3D muscle structure. Tissue depth pegs guide the reconstruction process based on average soft tissue depths for key anatomical landmarks from a contemporary living Egyptian population.
(image courtesy of Face Lab at Liverpool John Moores University)

3 Nasal aperture measurements guide the facial reconstruction process.
(image courtesy of Face Lab at Liverpool John Moores University)

well-documented Manchester method of reconstruction was followed (Wilkinson 2010). Without any evidence of Takabuti's ancestry, contemporary Egyptian data were selected as the most appropriate guidelines for soft tissue depths across the face (El-Mehallawi and Soliman 2001) (Fig. 2).

Facial features (eyes, eyebrows, nose, mouth, ears) were modelled following established anatomical and anthropometrical standards (Wilkinson 2010) (Fig. 3). Takabuti's skull suggested a soft, slightly upturned nose, full lips with a Cupid's bow shape, almond-shaped eyes and relatively large lower face proportions (Fig. 4).

A 3D print of the reconstruction was originally produced for the exhibition in the Ulster Museum (Fig. 5) which allowed for the application of painted skin textures along with synthetic eyeballs, a wig and replica jewellery. Takabuti was depicted based on her then bioanthropological profile, with estimated textures, such as dark brown eyes and moderately dark skin. Historical documentation was also utilised, suggesting the inclusion of a braided dark wig and eye make-up (typical of ancient Egyptian dress), as well as an ornate necklace.

Recently, two alternative updated 2D digital images were created in an attempt to portray Takabuti in a less stereotypical manner, depicting her natural hair, one without and one with typical ancient Egyptian make-up (Figs. 6 and 7). Only her hair has been depicted in colour, as this was well preserved, and all other 'textures' are presented in greyscale.

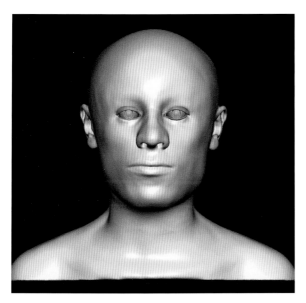

4 Final 3D facial reconstruction of Takabuti.
(image courtesy of Face Lab at Liverpool John Moores University)

6 The reconstructed face of Takabuti after photo editing software was used to add realistic skin and hair textures to create the facial depiction.
(image courtesy of Face Lab at Liverpool John Moores University)

5 Painted 3D print of the facial reconstruction of Takabuti on display at the Ulster Museum. A 3D print was produced in 2008 and hand painted, with acrylic eyeballs, false eyelashes, a wig and jewellery added.
(photograph courtesy of Eileen Murphy, Queen's University Belfast)

7 Takabuti depicted with stylised curly hair in a high chignon style, along with typical ancient Egyptian make-up.
(image courtesy of Face Lab at Liverpool John Moores University)

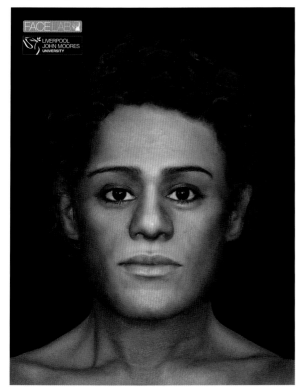

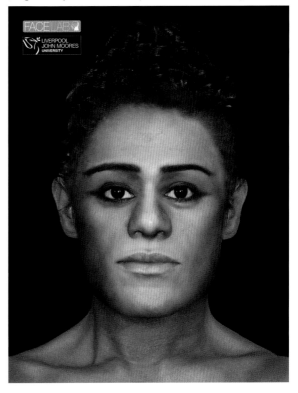

References

Brace, S., Diekmann, Y., Booth, T. J., Faltyskova, Z., Rohland, N., Mallick, S., Ferry, M., Michel, M., Oppenheimer, J., Broomandkhoshbacht, N., Stewardson, K., Walsh, S., Kayser, M., Schulting, R., Craig, O. E., Sheridan, A., Pearson, M. P., Stringer, C., Reich, D., Thomas M. G. and Barnes, I. 2019. Population replacement in Early Neolithic Britain. *Nature Ecology and Evolution* 3, 765–71.

Buti, L., Gruppioni, G. and Benazzi, S. 2017. Facial reconstruction of famous historical figures: between science and art. In C. M. Stojanowski and W. N. Duncan (eds), *Studies in Forensic Biohistory: Anthropological Perspectives*, pp. 191–212. Cambridge: Cambridge University Press.

El-Mehallawi, I. H. and Soliman, E. H. 2001. Ultrasonic assessment of facial soft tissue thicknesses in adult Egyptians. *Forensic Science International* 117, 99–107.

Swaney, M. and Balachandran, S. 2018. Who am I? Remembering the dead through facial reconstruction. http://archaeologicalmuseum.jhu.edu/the-collection/object-stories/who-am-i-remembering-the-dead-through-facial-reconstruction/ (last accessed 21 September 2020).

Wilkinson, C. 2010. Facial reconstruction – anatomical art or artistic anatomy? *Journal of Anatomy* 216, 235–50.

Takabuti – in Life, in Death and as Part of a Museum Collection

Rosalie David and Eileen Murphy

When we set out to compile this volume, we did so with the intent of sharing the story of Takabuti so that all those who visit her in the Ulster Museum could have an opportunity to learn more about her. For too long she has lain in her case with no voice, a woman out of her time, who has often provoked a very human response in those who visit her (Fig. 1).

We have introduced life in Egypt during the 25th Dynasty, when she would have lived, and considered what life would have been like for her as a relatively wealthy mistress of a household and daughter of a priest of Amun (Fig. 2). We also dealt with what we might consider a separate phase of her existence – her time in the various museums of Belfast from her first arrival in 1834 through to the present day. It is clear that she has continued to elicit wonder and provoke musings on ancient Egypt for museum visitors since that time.

1 Bouquet of flowers on the top of Takabuti's glass case left by an anonymous member of the public in August 1961, a reminder that these are the remains of a human being. (© National Museums NI, Collection Ulster Museum)

2 Artist's impression of
Takabuti enjoying musical
entertainment at home.
(Libby Mulqueeny, Queen's
University Belfast)

What Have We Learned since 1835?

The similarities between the questions posed by those who originally examined Takabuti's coffin and remains in 1835 and those posed by the twenty-first-century researchers involved in the Takabuti Project are striking. The Revd Dr Edward Hincks in 1835 did an excellent job of reading the hieroglyphs, to which we now add an explanation of the imagery on the sarcophagus by John Taylor. In 1835 it was identified that Takabuti was a petite young woman with somewhat European features, beautifully curled hair and a very healthy set of teeth. We can now expand upon this to say that she had unusual DNA with a rare mitochondrial haplogroup (H4a1), previously not reported for ancient Egypt, but identified in prehistoric individuals from the Canary Islands, Germany and Bulgaria (see Chapter 2, pp. 56–57). Her hair has been shown to have been cut around the time of death, and covered with a potentially sticky gel prior to styling in a curled high chignon. Her hair must have been an important part of her identity, since many of her contemporaries would have had shaven heads and worn wigs to avoid the discomfort of head lice. A possible louse egg was identified in Takabuti's hair, suggesting that she might have suffered such discomfort (see Chapter 2, pp. 60–64). No palaeopathological lesions were identified in Takabuti's skeleton and no evidence of disease was determined through state-of-the-art 'discovery' proteomics on a sample of her skeletal muscle tissue (see Chapter 3, p. 68; pp. 80–82). Modern dental analysis has confirmed the good condition and appearance of her teeth, while isotopic analysis has indicated that her diet was fairly constant in the months before she died and largely comprised temperate climate C3 crops such as wheat and barley (see Chapter 3, pp. 71–74; pp. 88–90).

In 1835 it was recorded that Takabuti's eyes had been removed and replaced with balls of material as part of the mummification process, but we now know that her eyeballs, as opposed to eye sockets, were packed with linen. We also know that her brain was not removed by breaking the delicate internal cranial bones via the nose as per standard practice, but rather that it was removed through the foramen magnum at the base of the cranium, and the cavity was then partly filled with a liquid, which may have comprised a composite containing pine resin, in addition to other more solid materials. The head was then surrounded by a supporting collar made of pine resin (see Chapter 4, pp. 100–101). They observed in 1835 that her chest and abdomen were full of dense aromatic packing material, and modern chemical analysis has revealed that this largely comprised sawdust from the cedar tree and liquified pine resin (see Chapter 4, pp. 108–10). She appears to have been eviscerated by means of two routes – a cut in her left flank and via the perineal area – both of which also provided access for insertion of the packing material. The heart – her ticket to the afterlife – has been identified in a wrapped package at the front of the chest (see Chapter 4, pp. 102–103). A large bundle of linen placed towards the back of the left side of the chest appears to have been used to pack a wound, and one of the most remarkable discoveries of the 2018–19 analysis has been the determination that Takabuti was murdered. She appears to have been struck on the back with force by an axe, causing a major wound that would have resulted in rapid death due to a collapsed lung and associated catastrophic bleeding (see Chapter 4, pp. 91–95; pp. 96–99).

Multidisciplinary studies offer many excellent opportunities for cooperative research, and produce a depth and breadth of information that would not otherwise be available. However, data collected in this way sometimes appears to provide contradictory results. In these instances, the interpretation becomes more difficult, and conflicting evidence has to be considered in the overall historical or archaeological context. In 1835 the Revd Dr Hincks dated Takabuti's coffin on the basis of stylistic features which he considered to indicate that she had lived around 2,000–2,500 years ago, and modern analysis of the coffin has firmly placed it in the 25th Dynasty. One of the most complex aspects of the modern investigation of Takabuti related to radiocarbon dating. Over the years this technique has raised many questions in Egyptology, and, although there have been considerable advances in the technology, contamination (which might have affected a sample at any time in its history) of mummified remains is an issue. Radiocarbon dating can produce results which are at variance with the historical, archaeological and inscriptional evidence. The range of radiocarbon dates obtained from samples taken from Takabuti's mummy and coffin have posed some interesting questions (see Chapter 2, pp. 44–47). The data demonstrate some of the complexities associated with the interpretation of results, particularly with regard to potential preservation and contamination issues relating to the wood and hair samples. The radiocarbon result for the wood sample from the coffin does not match the date provided by the stylistic and inscriptional analysis of the coffin. One interpretation of this mismatch could be that the mummy and the coffin do not belong together. However, the overall assessment of the scientific and archaeological evidence indicates that both the mummy and coffin most probably did belong to Takabuti, and that she lived and died in the 25th Dynasty.

The Egyptian Way of Attaining Eternity

According to the Egyptians' earliest religious beliefs, only the king, who was half-divine, could look forward to an individual afterlife; he was expected to join the gods in a sacred barque and sail around the heavens forever (Fig. 3). His subjects could only hope to achieve eternity vicariously, through his royal bounty. However, following the democratisation of religious beliefs during the Middle Kingdom (c. 2061–c. 1665 BC), the situation changed. It was believed that, although the king's afterlife continued as before, there was now an opportunity for everyone – whether rich or poor – to attain eternal life. This was dependent on fulfilling ethical and moral standards when alive, and the performance of correct burial procedures at the time of death.

3 The Valley of the Kings, Luxor. Most of the rulers of the 18th to 20th Dynasties were interred here, in tombs cut into the rock. In the 25th Dynasty, the Egyptian elite continued to be buried in nearby areas, but their Kushite rulers built their own pyramids far away in Nubia.
(photograph courtesy of Rosalie David, University of Manchester)

These beliefs were closely tied in with worship of the god Osiris. There is no extant record that Osiris was ever a human king, but it is clear that the ancient Egyptians believed that he was. According to their mythological texts, he was an early ruler of Egypt who was murdered and subsequently resurrected as a god to become the ruler and judge of an underworld kingdom situated just below the western horizon. Depending on a successful outcome to their divine interrogation on the Day of Judgement, even non-royals could expect to be admitted to this paradise.

The Day of Judgement is an important part of the *Book of the Dead* (known in antiquity as the *Book of Going Forth by Day*). These funerary papyri include declarations and spells intended to ease the owner's passage into the next world. Figure 4 shows a section of the *Book of the Dead* owned by the scribe Ani. He is led forward (far left) by the jackal-headed god of embalming, Anubis, to face his judgement. He recites the 'Negative Confession', affirming before the divine tribunal (top row) that he committed no major crimes or sins during his lifetime. His heart is matched against the feather (representing truth) in the pans of the balance; if he lies, it will weigh against him, and he will be thrown to the composite animal known as the 'Devourer', shown near the scales. However, the papyrus affirms that the gods find him innocent, and the falcon-headed Horus leads Ani into the presence of Osiris (far right), who is supported by the goddesses Nephthys (front) and Isis. Henceforth, Ani will pass his afterlife in the kingdom of Osiris.

The tomb itself was regarded as an alternative location where part of the afterlife could be spent. In this sacred space, carved and painted wall-scenes showed activities that would contribute to the deceased's enjoyment of the next life. Funerary equipment included figurines of servants and models of food production to provide infinite nourishment for the owner. Articles of everyday use included clothing, make-up

4 A section of the *Book of the Dead* owned by the scribe Ani. It depicts the weighing of Ani's heart at the Day of Judgement, and his ultimate acceptance and approval by the king and judge of the dead, Osiris. From Ani's tomb at Thebes, c. 1275–1250 BC. Purchased for the British Museum by Sir Wallis Budge in 1888.
(Creative Commons Attribution-ShareAlike International licence (CC BY 4.0) https://commons.wikimedia. org/wiki/File:Weighing_of_the_ heart.jpg)

5 Scene painted on a wooden sarcophagus c. 400 BC, showing Anubis, god of embalming and cemeteries, mummifying the deceased owner's body, which lies on a lion-headed bier. The four canopic jars under the bier were receptacles for the viscera removed from the body during the mummification procedure. (Creative Commons Attribution-ShareAlike licence (CC BY-SA 2.0), https://commons.wikimedia.org/wiki/File:WLANL_-_andrevanb_-_kist_uit_de_27-_31e_dynastie_(4).jpg)

and jewellery, and the coffins and mummy were regarded as a *locus* to which the deceased owner's spirit could return in order to receive spiritual nourishment. All these tomb elements were activated and 'brought to life' by the performance of magico-religious rituals (Fig. 5).

Despite their care and preparation for the afterlife, the Egyptians were aware that most tombs were ransacked, sometimes soon after burial had taken place. Once the integrity of the tomb and its contents was broken, their ability to facilitate the deceased owner's eternity was lost. This is of direct relevance to Takabuti's burial – the location of her tomb is unknown, the funerary goods that accompanied her final passage are long since gone, and her mummy now rests in a museum environment. According to Egyptian belief, the original conditions prepared for her afterlife no longer exist to provide the necessary protection for her physical remains and a residence for her spirit.

However, the Egyptians had another way of ensuring that the deceased passed into the next world. An individual's name was regarded as an integral and important part of their personal identity, and mentioning or repeating it was believed to ensure eternal existence. Indeed, ancient funerary texts asked the living to 'Say my name and I shall live'. Many people – including museum visitors and those who read this book – once again, in the twenty-first century, know and repeat Takabuti's name. Perhaps in this way we are giving her an alternative kind of eternity.

Endpiece

Takabuti's Legacy

David Tosh

Tucked away in the recesses of the Ulster Museum's store is a box. Inside is a wooden fragment of a coffin from the Atlantic island of St Helena. Although not ancient Egyptian in origin, it is associated with a man arguably responsible for Takabuti's arrival in Belfast – Napoleon. Without the French invasion of Egypt in 1798, it is unlikely that Takabuti would have found herself a resident of Belfast. Scientific expeditions in the early nineteenth century led to stories of ancient Egyptian culture spreading across Europe. Northern Ireland and its inhabitants were not immune to 'Egyptomania', and one Holywood, Co. Down, resident, Thomas Greg, succumbed to the allure of the stories and visited Egypt. Takabuti's arrival in Belfast was a symptom of the wider desire among society, and the excitement she caused then remains, to some degree, to this day.

Although not Takabuti's first home in Belfast, the Ulster Museum is now where she resides. Resting in the darkness of the museum's Egyptian Gallery, Takabuti's presence is inextricably linked to the museum's identity. She remains one of the most identifiable and sought after 'objects' for visitors. Although marketed as a reason to visit the Ulster Museum, advertising alone cannot explain her popularity. Could it be the role she plays in maintaining Northern Ireland's awareness of Egyptology, and her particular role in introducing children to the topic? Ancient Egypt has been a subject for primary school children in Northern Ireland for no less than 30 years. Since at least the 1990s the Ulster Museum has used its Egyptian collection to support the curriculum, and every year over 4,000 school children visit the museum to learn about ancient Egypt. For many of these children it will be their first, and sometimes only, visit to the Ulster Museum until they return as parents themselves.

The exciting and sometimes frightening experience of coming face to face with history brings ancient Egypt alive for many children and remains an abiding memory for years. This experience is shared by visitors returning to the Ulster Museum, and by participants in the museum's outreach programmes. For some this will be the spark that ignites an interest that will lead to the pursuit of a career, while, for others, it will prompt a lifelong interest in Egyptology.

Takabuti's importance in sustaining interest in ancient Egypt is arguably not limited to Belfast or Northern Ireland. Within the context of the island of Ireland, Takabuti is an important ambassador for ancient Egypt, as her home is one of only two locations on the island where mummies can be seen. Without the National Museum of Ireland in Dublin or the Ulster Museum, there would be nowhere in Ireland where members of the public can get so close to a face from the past. There are other Egyptian collections, and other mummies are held behind closed doors, but only Dublin and Belfast provide opportunities for the public to see the remains of someone who lived thousands of years ago. Some might argue that this is a continuation of Victorian freak shows, but I would argue that mummies show visitors that they were people too. This is important, as it provides an opportunity for people to connect with Egyptian collections in a way that alabaster pots or faience scarabs do not. Compared to Britain, where over 30 museums have mummies on display, the opportunity to share this experience and imagine who the person was are few for the people of Ireland. The fact that Takabuti has been the face of ancient Egypt in Ireland for over 185 years emphasises her important role as an ambassador.

It is National Museums Northern Ireland's hope that this book will add to the interest in ancient Egypt that Takabuti already generates. The book is an example of the contribution that Takabuti continues to make to the Ulster Museum and the wider world of Egyptology. We hope that, as technology further advances and our understanding of ancient Egypt grows, Takabuti will continue to reveal more insights into the life she lived all those years ago.

Index